ROCK THiS!

chris
ROCK

rock THiS!

 HYPERION

NEW YORK

Library of Congress Cataloging-in-Publication Data

Rock, Chris.
    Rock this! / Chris Rock.
      p.   cm.
    ISBN 0-7868-6289-0
    I. Title.
  PN6162.R617   1997
  818'.5402—dc21   97–21453
                          CIP

Designed by Jill Gogal

FIRST EDITION
10 9 8 7 6 5 4 3 2 1

For my dad, Julius Rock.
The funniest guy I've ever known.

ACKNOWLEDGMENTS

Many thanks to my wife, Malaak, and my family, and to Pamela Johnson, Dan Strone, Laurie Abkemeier, Merry Harper, Michael Rotenberg, Nelson George, Nick Frenkel, Mark Landesman, and my main man, Little Penny.

CONTENTS

SPECIAL THANKS

I think I'm supposed to say something really great here about writer David Rensin, who helped me turn my observations into a real book. At least that's what he says I'm supposed to do. But the way I look at it is this: **He got to work with me on this book**. That's the ultimate compliment, isn't it?

RENSIN: Come on, Chris. You have to say at least one nice thing.

ME: Uh, okay. You're right. Lemme see . . . So, David, what other stuff have you worked on?

RENSIN: I co-wrote *The Bob Book: A Celebration of the Ultimate Okay Guy*. It's a best-selling humorous sociology of men named Bob.

ME: That's white.

RENSIN: I helped Jeff Foxworthy write *No Shirt. No Shoes. . . . No Problem!*

ME: That's white.

RENSIN: I've been working on the autobiography of Larry Sanders, with Garry Shandling.

ME: Hmmm. Also white. Anything else?

RENSIN: I did *Blending In: My First Winter in Aspen*. Sort of a first person account of . . .

ME: . . . white people.

RENSIN: And don't forget *Everything You Ever Wanted to Know about Salt*.

ME: That's *very* white.

RENSIN: And, well, I'm not supposed to tell anyone, but I ghost-wrote *Prescription for Love: The Autobiography of Bernie Kopell.* You know, the doctor on "The Love Boat."

ME: Got it. Okay, I know what to say:

"No white man in America better understands the plight of the black man than David Rensin."*

RENSIN: Thanks, Chris. That's very white of you.

*Actually, no one better understands the plight of comedians trying to write books than David Rensin.

Every comedian has a moment in his life when he realizes he's a little bit different from everyone else. It's like being the only guy in a movie who sees the ghost. The ghost talks to you and you talk to him. Then you turn to your friend and say, "Hey. Do you see that ghost?" And he says, "What ghost?"

ROCK THiS!

Can you believe it? These messages were on my answering machine yesterday:

"Hello, Chris? It's Oprah Winfrey. I'm calling to let you know I've always been a fan of your work, especially that part in I'm Gonna Git You Sucka *when you asked Isaac Hayes, 'How much for one rib?' Everyone at my company, HARPO—that's Oprah spelled backward—loved it.*

"Listen, thanks for sending me a copy of your new book, Rock This! *I really loved it—although I think if you wanted to sell books you should have put my name in the title. Maybe something like,* Love Letter to Oprah.

"Anyway, even though I really liked the book, I'm sorry to say that I'm going to have to turn you down for the 'Oprah Winfrey Book Club.' It's not because I didn't like the book—which, as I just said, I did. I thought it was quite funny, insightful, and intelligent.

"But I have to level with you: We at 'Oprah' are Sinbad people. We always have been and always will be. Do you remember Sinbad's HBO special where he did that joke about the worst thing you can say to your wife?

" 'Baby, your butt looks good.'

"This is a big butt show. Lots of big butt women tune in. Let me check—no, my butt is small these days. But I still think Sinbad is one of the most talented people alive. He's more than a comedian; he's a great actor, and I don't get to see enough of

him. I think he should get more major screen roles. Just between us, I thought Sinbad should have played Malcolm X. I was in one of my houses the other day watching Driving Miss Daisy and I was just sitting there thinking, it's a good movie and all, but I couldn't help wondering why Sinbad wasn't driving Miss Daisy. When I watched Pulp Fiction, John Travolta was good. Sam Jackson was excellent. But wouldn't you just love to have seen Sinbad as a hit man? Come to think of it, Spike Lee's about to do The Jackie Robinson Story. Who would make a better Jackie than Sinbad?

"You know, a couple years from now when I buy ABC from the Disney Company, I'm not just going to give Sinbad his own show, I'm going to give him his own night.

"Forget Must See TV. Must See Sinbad.

"One other thing. Level with me. Did you really write this? I mean if you did, great. But if you didn't write it or you can't write, don't be ashamed. There are places you can go for help. You needn't suffer in silence. My great-great-grandmother couldn't write very well. For instance, here's a passage from a letter she once sent me: 'I buv ooo.' But even though she lacked basic language skills, just from that little passage, I could tell that she cared for me.

"I can tell you're also a caring person by the tone of your book—even though it is confrontational in a way that often made we wonder, 'Can't we all just get along?'

"Look, Chris, I've got to go. I'm sorry I can't use your book on the 'Oprah Winfrey Book Club.' Maybe you can still be a guest on the show sometime. Let us know where you'll be during the next few months and we'll call you. Stay in touch. But if you ever write a book about Sinbad, please contact us immediately."

* BEEP *

"Yeah, Chris, Ricki Lake here. Read your book. I can't say I loved it, but then again, I'm not much of a reader. The first thing I want to ask you is: did you really write it? It had a lot of big words in it. Like 'criteria.' I guess it's not really that big a word, it's just that I don't use it very often.

"Chris, I want to tell you I've always been a big fan. I loved you in I'm Gonna Git You Sucka, especially the scene where you ask Isaac Hayes, 'How much for one rib?' I have to tell you though, I'm not going to be able to have you on 'The Ricki Lake Show.' And it's not because I don't like you. I actually think you're kind of cute.

"See, we on 'The Ricki Lake Show,' we, uh, well . . . I'll just come right out and say it: We don't do books. My audience is visually oriented. Some of them have problems with their cognitive skills—did I just say 'cognitive'? That's a big word. I gotta write that down.

"And it's not a race issue. Even though I'm white, we at 'The Ricki Lake Show' like black men and women. Some of our most entertaining guests are black. It's really just that—I don't know how to say this—my producers think you're a little too advanced for my audience. They aren't really comfortable with smart black people.

"If it were up to me, things might be different, but I don't own my show. I'm not the producer. Besides, that's not the point.

"You know, when I first heard you wanted to be on the show, I was so happy. Then I saw a recent picture of you and realized you didn't have the Jheri curl anymore. We at 'The Ricki Lake Show' love Jheri curls. Then I heard you were married. So I thought we could use that angle. Then I found out your wife is black and really beautiful. Now, if you had married a trailer-trash white girl who weighed three hundred sixty-three pounds and had an interesting eating disorder, we would bump tomorrow's guests to get you on. But as things stand, I don't see you fitting into our plans.

"However, I'm not closing the door on your being on the show. If in the next few months you get a Jheri curl, marry an extremely fat white woman, or lose a few trillion brain cells, look us up. We'd love to have you."

* BEEP *

Life is strange. Anyway, thanks for buying my book. You did buy it, right? Well, what are you waiting for? Go pay the money right now. Then we'll be cool. You pay, and we'll go out for some ribs.

Well, one rib.

Come on. Buy the book.

In the words of Little Penny, "Could you do that for a brother?"

ROCK THiS!

WE ALL LOOK THE SAME IN THE DARK

The country's in an uproar. Everybody's mad at each other.

It's sad.

Black people are mad. White people are mad.

Black people yell racism.

White people yell reverse racism.

Chinese people yell sideways racism.

Just what is reverse racism? Is there something white people are *not* getting? Is there a job a white man didn't get yesterday? Reverse racism is like Mike Tyson saying, "It's not fair; me always having to fight the heavy guys. From now on, I only want to fight lightweights."

* * *

Whenever the white man's got me down, I turn on the TV and watch boxing. White guys cannot box. Black guys fight better than white guys, Puerto Rican guys box better than black guys, and so on. I guess the lower you are on the socioeconomic ladder, the better you fight. I bet for every Puerto Rican fighter, there's an American Indian waiting to kick his ass.

I feel bad about the American Indians. We took—wait a minute, *white people* took—their land. Now they have very little left. And everything exploits the Indians. There was "F-Troop," the Mazola commercial, the Atlanta Braves, and the Cleveland Indians. And during football season, they have to hear about the Washington Redskins. That's like having a team named the Newark Niggers.

Remember the Indian chief with the tear in his eye, supposedly crying for the environment? He wasn't crying for the environment; he was crying because somebody took his land, then fucked and killed his wife.

The ozone was the least of his worries.

Since the Indians got swindled over some beads, nobody in America has been too excited about newcomers. Every racial and ethnic group gets treated like shit when they get here—by the racial and ethnic group that got treated like shit when they came in on the earlier flight. Nobody says, "Hey, here are the new guys. Let's welcome them. Let's bake a cake for the Irish."

A COUNTRY DiViDED

People act as if there's the possibility of a real race war. They say the country's divided over race. Split in half.

Bullshit.

Black people are only 12 percent of this country's population. Twelve percent isn't half! You can't have a race war when it's 88 percent versus 12 percent.

We'd lose!

We're in New York, L.A., D.C., Chicago, Atlanta. Maybe ten places altogether. Have you ever been to Montana? Not a lot of brothers there. Not too many black people in Minnesota, aside from Prince and Kirby Puckett.

In New York, sure. We're half the city. But upstate, the only place you'll find more blacks than whites is in Attica.

I've been to every state in the union. There's *a lot* of white people out there. But some militant black people still make noises like, "Hey, we should just take over."

Forget it. Malcolm X counted up them and us. Then he said, "Oh, shit. We could try, but I think we might get *fucked* up."

Unless the race war takes place in a boxing ring, one guy at a time.

THE BLACK EXPERiENCE

Sometimes I hate life because I was born a suspect. All black men are born suspects. When I came out of my mother, right away, if anything happened within a three-block radius, I was a suspect. As a matter of fact, the day I was born, somebody's car got stolen from the hospital parking lot. They made me stand in a lineup. That was pretty tough, considering I wasn't even a day old and couldn't crawl, much less walk. Good thing I had a couple black nurses to help hold me up. I got lucky. They were in the lineup, too.

If you're born a suspect, everybody's scared of you. I can walk down the street anywhere in America and women will clutch their purses tighter, hold on to their Mace, and lock their car doors. If I look up into the windows of the apartments I pass by I can see old ladies on the phone. They've already dialed 9-1-... and are just waiting for me to do something wrong.

* * *

Most black people I know have felt the consequences of racism: bad neighborhoods, bad services, crime. But in the black community they're just part of life. We notice, but we don't really notice.

To feel real in-your-face racism—to be called a nigger and be treated bad, bad, bad—we have to go to where white people live and vacation. Like the Hamptons. The only black people around are those working for white people. Walk into a store and if you're black, no one says hello. They say, "What do you want?" as in "What the hell are you doing here and how soon are you leaving?"

If you're black and have money—if you buy the house and live in the white neighborhood—you feel it even more.

I had a white friend who used to go to downtown Brooklyn with his brother. They'd go into a store and wait until a group of black kids came in. Immediately, security started following the black group. That's when my white friend and his brother just started taking whatever they wanted. They didn't even have to hide it. They'd walk out wearing coats with price tags hanging down.

A message to store owners: "That's right. Better keep watching those black kids."

I'm always afraid of those stores where they have to buzz you in. I'm concerned that they won't buzz me in. Then I'll just have to stand there feeling like shit. My fantasy is to go up to one of these fancy boutiques on Fifth Avenue, take a brick out of my coat, and throw it through the fucking window.

And then I'll write them a big fat check that not only covers it but also pays for everybody's lunch.

Of course, I won't ever *really* do that because I avoid those stores. Black people stay away from a lot of stuff where white people are in charge. A lot of us don't vote. We go to the doctor less. We're intimidated by institutions.

Hmm. I think it started with the institution of **slavery**.

WE ALL LOOK THE SAME iN THE DARK

White people don't know how to tell the difference between one black man and another. If they could, we'd all get along. It would solve everything. But to the white man, we're all the same.

Trouble.

They see two black men together and it's a crowd. A dangerous mob. To white people, even Ed Bradley and Bryant Gumbel hanging out, waiting to cross the street together, is potentially scary. Clarence Thomas in an Adidas warm-up suit will *not* get a cab in Washington, D.C. He *will* get followed around in the mall while he tries to check out athletic footwear.

White people are so blind that they can't even tell the difference between me and a larger-than-life character like Suge Knight. But my friends, there's a **BIG FUCKING DIFFERENCE.** You can tell just by looking that one of us is not to be fucked with.

Blacks, however, can immediately distinguish between white guys. For instance: Pauly Shore and J.F.K., Jr.

See what I mean? You know immediately.

Why is this so? Because blacks have *had* to learn to differentiate. We're confronted by white faces on TV. We pay our rent to a white guy. We work for white guys. White people don't have to know anything about black people to survive. They can go their whole lives and never even know a black person.

Black people have gone to the Olympics for years, representing America. Not black people, but America. That's the problem with black people. We want to be down. We want to be cool. When other ethnic groups get dissed they form their *own* communities.

Chinese people came over here. They got dissed. They said, "Fuck you! We got Chinatown. All right? Our own thing."

Italian people came over here. They got dissed. They said, "Yo man, fuck you! Little Italy. All right? We got our own thing."

You ever heard of Little Africa?

Didn't think so.

Little Africa is the GHETTO.

Let's see: I don't think we created the ghetto on purpose.

Black people have it bad. At least the Chinese and Italians have their own restaurants.

That's right. We don't even have our own food. Soul food is *not* black food. It's just some nasty shit they fed to the slaves. You think a ham hock tasted good the first time the white man shoved it in our faces? No. We had to cover it in seasoning to make it work. Black people don't even have salad dressing— and *everybody* has salad dressing, even Paul Newman. Our salad dressing is hot sauce.

HELP WANTED: ONE LEADER. PLEASE APPLY WiTHiN

Things would get better for black people if we could just get a leader. We need a leader. We need one bad. We need someone who is recognized by everyone. Someone undisputed and unanimous. We need a man we can point to and say, "He's the guy."

But it's a very hard position to fill. Everybody who had the job before got shot in the head.

POTENTIAL LEADER: Oh, how'd the last guy do? Why did he leave? Did he get another job?

US: Kinda . . . you could say that.

It's hard to fill that vacancy. Harder than selling Nicole Brown's condo. It doesn't matter how many benefits you give.

US: We got dental.
POTENTIAL LEADER: That's all right. I'll pass.

But we still need a black leader. Someone qualified. Someone who won't just beg for money from white people. But even if the job weren't dangerous, every candidate has something wrong with him. There's always a catch. I'm talking about major flaws. Let's break it down:

Al Sharpton: I'm sure he's done a lot of good things for the community, but when you bring up his name people act as if he's a comedic punch line.

"Why'd the chicken cross the road?"

"Al Sharpton!"

He looks like Bookman from "Good Times," with a damn perm. How can you take anyone seriously with that hair? No matter what he says, you can't take your eyes off the hair. If Al Sharpton said he could cure AIDS, you'd say, "Right. Look at that hair."

Jesse Jackson: We can't question his credentials: marched with Dr. King, a leader in the Civil Rights movement. But what happened to Jesse? Jesse was real *for a minute*. He ran for President, had some influence. Then it got out of hand. He'd run, then not run. Run, then not run. He couldn't make up his mind. Next, he started rhyming just a little too much. Just got silly.

"Education. Procreation. Be a man. I like ham."

I thought maybe he was making an album with Puffy.

Then he stopped preaching. Jesse used to be a reverend, right? But when was the last time you saw Jesse in church? The man's *never* in church. He's on TV.

I went to a Tyson fight one Saturday night. You know what fights are like in Vegas? Nothing but pimps, prostitutes, drug dealers, and naked ring girls holding up the round placards. The most sleazy thing. Not a godly atmosphere. And there was Jesse sitting next to me. I turned to him and said, "It's Saturday night. Ain't church tomorrow?"

Louis Farrakhan: Good organizational skills. The man who brought us the Million Man March. But Farrakhan has a problem with the Jews. Can this help us?

It's not really constructive. Besides, I don't get it. The only way you can get over is to hate *nobody*.

I'm around brothers every day, all the time, and I've *never ever* heard a bunch of black people talking about Jews. Never.

Black people don't hate **Jews**.

Black people hate white people.

Just because we can tell the difference between one white guy and another doesn't mean we have time to dice them up into little groups.

"The Jews are fucked up, but Irish are cool."

You're *all* white to us.

The problem with all our black leaders is that their consciousness is defined by their views of white people.

If white people didn't exist, most black leaders would be out of work.

A lot of people ask me why I don't include Colin Powell when I mention black leaders. To be a true black leader, you have to be self-made. The fact that he was chairman of the Joint Chiefs of Staff makes him the equivalent of a sitcom in a good time slot. Is "Suddenly Susan" any good? We don't know. It's on after "Seinfeld."

No matter how you feel about Louis Farrakhan, Al Sharpton, or Jesse Jackson, they stand on their own. Nobody gave them what they have.

* * *

If there's any disagreement between blacks and Jews it's over which was worse: the Holocaust or slavery.

I'll tell you which was worse: It's a tie. Except for one thing. The Holocaust was illegal. Afterward, the Allies got to arrest people, lay blame, hold trials, and have a sense of closure.

Slavery was legal. No closure. Just over. As far as America is concerned, slavery and segregation were fads, just like pet rocks and disco.

Was there ever an apology?

I'd like one.

Reparations?

That's okay now, but at the time it would have been justice.

The Civil War was nice, but in the real history books it wasn't about slavery. It was about taxes.

Slavery affected the black psyche. Now, we're like Ron Goldman's father without a criminal "guilty" verdict. We're like battered wives ordered to stay with their husbands.

No wonder we're fucked up.

A CREATIVE SOLUTION

We still need a black leader. What are we going to do?

They import basketball players from Africa. How about bringing in one of those kings? They ran a country. We need a leader who already ran something. But we never get that guy. We get the *next* guy. Martin Luther King got shot—Jesse was standing right next to him.

"Let's use him."

As far as I'm concerned our leader doesn't even have to be black. Let's get Pat Riley. He's led a lot of black men to championships. Maybe he can take us to the promised land.

Having no leader has taken its toll. Now we're preoccupied with entertainers.

"You're role models. You have to act right."

Why does the public expect entertainers to behave better than everybody else?

It's ridiculous.

No one gave a fuck that Babe Ruth was an alcoholic. That was his problem. When Dwight Gooden got hooked on coke, that was his problem. It fucked with their teams, but it's not like they let the *community* down. They let themselves down. They're not thinking about you. They shouldn't be thinking about you. They should be thinking about getting off that shit.

Of course, this is just for *black* entertainers. You don't see anyone telling Jerry Seinfeld he's a good role model. Why? Because everyone *expects* whites to behave themselves. Goes with being white, I guess. But blacks . . .

In the old days, a black entertainer was just that: a black entertainer. He sang his song and that was it. No one cared about what he was doing offstage. It was his business. In the old days Sammy Davis, Jr., could fuck a white girl, snort some cocaine, get his eye knocked out, and it was cool. It was no reflection on black people. It was *his* business.

Nowadays, you've got to be an entertainer *and* a leader. It's too much. Rappers get shot and the people are all overcome. I loved Tupac and Biggie, but don't act like it's bigger than it is. Let's not blow it out of proportion.

"Biggie Smalls was *assassinated.* Tupac Shakur was *assassinated.*"

They weren't assassinated.

Martin Luther King was assassinated.

Malcolm X was assassinated.

The *Kennedy*s were assassinated.

Those brothers just **got shot**! They had some beefs. They're not here anymore. But don't make it bigger than it is.

I love Tupac and Biggie, but school is still going to be open on their birthdays. There won't be any pictures of the two hanging in Grandma's kitchen.

"Gramma, is that . . . Biggie? What was he like?"

WHO YOU CALLiNG RACiST?

Who's more racist: black people or white people?

Black people.

You know why? Because black people hate black people, too. Everything *white* people don't like about black people, *black* people don't like about black people. It's like our own personal civil war.

On one side, there's black people.

On the other, you've got niggers.

The niggers have got to go. Everytime black people want to have a good time, niggers mess it up. You can't do anything without some ignorant-ass niggers fucking it up.

Can't keep a disco open more than three weeks. Grand opening? Grand closing.

Can't go to a movie the first week it opens. Why? Because niggers are shooting at the screen.

"This movie is so good I gotta bust a cap in here."

I love black people, but I hate niggers. I am tired of niggers. I wish they would let me join the Ku Klux Klan. I'd do a drive-by from L.A. to Brooklyn.

You can't have anything valuable when you're around niggers. You can't have a big-screen TV. Well, you can have it, but you better move it in at three o'clock in the morning, paint it white, and hope niggers think it's a bassinet.

You can't have anything in your house. Why? Because the niggers who live next door will break in, take it all, and then come over the next day and go, "We heard ya got robbed."

"You know because *you* robbed me. You weren't hearing shit because you were *doing* shit."

I'm tired of niggers. Tired, tired, tired.

Niggers always want credit for some shit they're *supposed* to do. They'll brag about some stuff a normal man *just does*. They'll say something like, "Yeah? Well, I take care of my kids."

You're supposed to, you dumb motherfucker.

"I ain't never been ta jail."

Whaddya want? A cookie? You're not supposed to go to jail, you low-expectation-having motherfucker.

The worst thing about niggers is that they love to *not know*. Nothing makes a nigger happier than not knowing the answer to your question.

YOU: What's the capital of Zaire?
NIGGER: I don't know that shit.
YOU: Why the hell not?
NIGGER: Don't know.
YOU: Don't know?
NIGGER: Just keep'n it real.

Niggers love to keep it real. Real dumb. Next time niggers break into your house, if you want to save your money, put it in your books. Niggers don't read. Books are like kryptonite to a nigger.

YOU: Here. Read this book.
NIGGER: NOOOOOOOOO!

I'm tired of their shit. Our kids can't play anywhere. Every year the space gets smaller.

"Okay, you can go between that corner and that corner.

Okay, that's too far. Now you can go between that gate and that gate."

By the time the kid's ten she's just hopping in circles.

I'm tired, tired, tired. Fee-fie-foe-figure, boy do I hate a nigger.

Now the politicians are trying to get rid of welfare. Every time you see a welfare story on the news, you always see black people. Hey! Black people don't give a fuck about welfare. But niggers are shaking in their boots.

"They gonna take our shit!"

A black man who works two jobs, every day, hates a nigger on welfare.

"Nigger, get a job. I got two, you can't get one? I would give your lazy ass one of mine, but then you'd get fucked up, get laid off, and they wouldn't hire another nigger for ten years."

A black woman, with two kids, going to work every day, busting her ass, hates a bitch with nine kids collecting welfare. All she thinks is: "Bitch, stop fucking. Stop fucking! Stop it. Put the dick down. Get a job. Yes, you can get a job. Get a job holding dicks. But whatever you do, *get paid to do it.*"

I know what all you black readers think.

"Man, why you got to say that? Why you got to say that? It isn't us, it's the *media*. The media has distorted our image to make us look bad. Why must you come down on us like that, brother? It's not us, it's the media."

Please cut the shit. When I go to the money machine at night, I'm not looking over my shoulder for the media.

I'm looking for niggers.

Ted Koppel never took anything from me. Niggers have. Do you think I've got three guns in my house because the media's outside my door trying to bust in?

"Oh shit. It's Mike Wallace. Run!"

MOMMY? CAN i SAY "NiGGER?"

I just said "nigger" a whole lot. You probably think I shouldn't use the N-word, but that rule is just for white folks. Any black person can say "nigger" and get away with it. It's true. It's like calling your kid an idiot. Only *you* can call your kid that. Someone else calls your kid an idiot, there's a fight.

Yet some white people still wonder why black people can say "nigger" and they can't. Believe it or not, it's a very common question. I hear it all the time.

WHITE PERSON: Chris, can I say "nigger?"

ME: Why would you even *want* to?

WHITE PERSON: I don't mean anything *bad* by it. I've traveled the world, I got a yacht, I fucked Raquel Welch. Now, if I could just say "nigger," everything would be complete.

ME: No. After I smack you upside the head everything will be complete.

"Nigger" is one of those words, like "fuck," that means different things depending on how you use it.

"I love you, nigger." Good.

"You're my nigger." That's nice.

"Shut up, nigger!" Not so good.

"I'm going to kill you, nigger." You better run.

Of course, "nigger" is just a word. White people could call us anything, like "butter."

"Hey, you fucking butter! Pick that cotton, butter!"

The problem is that then they wouldn't be able to use the word "butter" for anything else. But they've got to use *something*. Next thing you know, white folks are sitting around the breakfast table with their eggs and toast, saying, "You're kidding. I can't believe it's *not* nigger."

THE MOST RACIST GUY IN THE WORLD

Who are the most racist people in the world?

Old black men.

A brother in his sixties hates everybody.

He can't stand white people. Why? Because old black men went through *real racism*. He didn't go through that "I can't get a cab" shit. He *was* the cab. The white man would jump on his back and say, "Main Street."

An old black man also hates young black people. To him, they've fucked up everything he's worked for.

But when an old black man sees an old white man, the old black man always kisses the old white man's ass.

"How you doing, sir? Pleased to meet you. Whatever I can getcha, you let me know."

But as soon as the white man walks out of sight, the black man starts up:

"Crack-ass cracker . . . put my foot in his cracker ass, crack-ass cracker. I wish that cracker would have said some shit to me. Lick my ass, fat-ass cracker, motherfucker, saltine cracker."

But when the white man comes back, it's, "Howdy, sir."

I have a 55-year-old uncle who *hates* white people. But he's married to a white lady. Can you believe it? He sits around going, "These crackers ain't shit . . . 'cept for Susie." He tried to explain the whole thing to me: "I got a white wife. So what? I love her, she loves me, that's all that matters. But I tell you this, if the revolution ever comes, I'll kill her first—just to show everybody I mean business."

He really said that.

I guess that's what O.J. was up to. He thought the revolution had already come.

COLOR CODING

No matter where I go, I always see signs of racism and racial imbalance.

For instance, white guys have quality dirty magazines like *Playboy, Penthouse,* and *Club.* What do black guys have? *Players* magazine, the lowest, nastiest publication on the face of the earth. The pictures aren't even in focus. They show a bunch of black girls getting off the toilet, trying to shield their faces. It's like the women are saying, "Hey, what are you doing in here? Are you crazy? What's wrong with you, you pervert?" I guess they don't even bother to ask permission to take the picture in the first place.

In *Playboy,* the women are posed sensually, like they're happy and getting paid. In *Players,* the women look mad, like they're only getting ten dollars and their pimp is taking eight.

In *Playboy,* the women don't have a blemish on their bodies. In *Players,* the model's got stretch marks from the eight kids she's had, plus the bullet wound from that time she got shot in the ass.

It's the same when you look at a white porno flick and compare it to a black porno flick. The white one's got actors, actresses, a plot, and even some extras who keep their clothes on—people who walk through, or hang around, who aren't even having sex.

A black porno flick is the sorriest thing on earth. No actors, no actresses, just a bunch of people sitting in a hotel room waiting for somebody to yell, "Action."

When somebody does, there's an argument.

Sometimes you'll pick up a black porno flick and with luck get a *real* actor—some out-of-work brother that you used to see on TV. You'll be watching and you'll say, "Hey wait a minute, isn't that Sticks from 'Happy Days'?"

Before I moved out of my parents' house and got my own place, my mother would sometimes clean up my room. Whenever she did, she used to take away all my dirty magazines.

When your mother takes your magazines, you can't say anything about it. You have to play it off like they were never there in the first place. She doesn't say anything, you don't say anything.

But you know it's happened because you're sitting around eating breakfast with your mother and there's this tension at the table. You both know you're not her little baby anymore.

You're like some pervert she's given birth to.

So you try to break the silence by asking a question:

"Mom, have you seen my baseball glove?"

And your mother goes, "No. Maybe you left it in the *Penthouse.*"

Sometimes you don't realize your mother has taken your stuff until it's too late. It's three o'clock in the morning, and your sexually explicit material is gone, just when you need it most. So you have to search the whole house for *anything* with a picture of a woman on it.

Pretty soon you're at the pantry, staring at a box of Aunt Jemima.

Get the box down. Look at her. Now she's looking at you. Your imagination kicks into gear and Aunt Jemima starts looking real good. She's young now. She takes that rag off her head, her hair touches the ground. Her big buttermilk breasts are hanging; she's got a big fat ass. And she starts talking to you in a real sexy voice.

"Come on, baby, let your auntie suck it. Come on, baby, put some syrup on that bad boy."

But right when you're ready to explode, Uncle Ben jumps off his box and says, "Leave her alone. That's my woman."

SUPERMARKET SWEEPSTAKES

I see inequality everywhere. For instance, ever notice how every city has two malls? The white mall, and the mall the white people *used* to go to. *That* mall must be something awful to actually *keep* white people from going.

"It's too black in here."

White people like black people the way they like their seasoning: Just a dash.

I hate the black mall. There is nothing in the black mall but sneakers and baby clothes. I guess that's all they think we're doing: running and fucking. Fifteen sneaker stores: Footlocker, Athlete's Foot, Foot in Your Ass. In the white mall they have big-ass stores. Valet parking. Personal shoppers.

In the black mall, there's no Macy's, no Saks. Just an eight-story Woolworth with personal shoppers who say, "Can I help you with your *cheap shit*?"

Yet these days all you hear is, "Gotta shop black. Keep it in the community." It's easy to shop black if all you want is a pack of potato chips.

The only thing worse than the black mall is the black market. Forget the word "super." Hell, I don't even know why they've got the word "market" in there. When I was a kid my mother used to drive an hour to get food and I never knew why, until I grew up.

White people have nice supermarkets. Inviting supermarkets. In the white supermarket, the nice doors slide open, you step in, and a cool breeze hits your face. It's lovely. The whole place says, "Come on in."

All the white people reading this book: next time you go to the market, kiss your grocer.

In the black supermarket the doors are always fucked up. You have to jump on the electric pad two or three times to get them open. Now and then the doors will hit back and smack you in the head. It's almost as if they know you're broke. When you get in, a hot, hot breeze hits you in the face and the place is dark. Half the lights don't work. Some markets don't even have lights—only skylights. When the sun goes down, the supermarket is closed.

There's nothing fresh in a black supermarket, unless you count "fresh from the can." There's no red meat. The meat is brown. And if you do get some red meat, you better cook it *that* day because it's gonna be spoiled tomorrow. You'll wake up and locusts will be having a convention on the meat—and all because you wanted to shop black.

All the fruits are nasty, too. Flies circle around the fruit and even the flies aren't new. Sometimes the grocer sticks in plastic fruit to try and fool you—and the flies. If you can get an apple, it's got a worm in it.

And the worm is dead.

WHY DO YOU THiNK THEY CALL iT "SCHOOL"?

Sometimes I think I need to go back to school. But the problem is that if you're black, you get more respect for going to jail than for going to school. You come out of jail and you're the fucking *man*. You come out of school, nobody cares.

"Hey, I just graduated from high school."

"So what, ya punk-ass bitch. Don't come around with all that reading and shit. Don't come around with all that counting and shit. I can count too: one, two, four, five, nine . . . so what?"

You could have a master's degree. Niggers don't care.

"I got my master's."

"What? You my master now? I'm supposed to listen to your punk ass? Fuck you, nigger. So what if you got your master's degree? You the smarty-ass nigger? So, let me ask you this: Can you kick *my* ass?"

I dropped out of school. Sorry. I guess I'm not the best role model. Later, I got a G.E.D. You know what G.E.D. stands for? Good-Enough Diploma. A G.E.D. is bullshit. I don't get it. You mean I can make up four years in six hours? When you get a G.E.D., someone always has the nerve to say, "*Now* you can go to college."

Hey, you can't go to a *real* college with a G.E.D. The only place that will take you is a community college. You know why they call it community college? Because it's like a disco with books. Anybody in the community can go: Crackheads, prostitutes, drug dealers. "Come on in!"

I once took a black history class. I figured since I'm black I already knew everything. I figured I'd pass just by showing up.

Failed it.

Isn't that sad, a black man failing black history? But I didn't know anything about Africa. When you go to white schools you learn about Europe up the ass, but you don't learn that much about Africa. The only thing I know about Africa is that it's far, far away. A 35-hour flight. Imagine the boat ride. The boat ride's so long there's still slaves on their way here.

All I learned in school about being black was Martin Luther King. That's all they ever teach. Martin Luther King. He was the answer to everything.

TEACHER: What's the capital of Zaire?
ME: Martin Luther King.

TEACHER: Tell us the name of the woman who would not give up
her seat on the bus.

ME: Oh, that's hard. Are ya sure it was a woman? Okay, I
got it: Mar*tina* Luther King."

You know what's sad? Martin Luther King stood for non-violence. Now that he's dead he stands for a holiday and a street. Martin Luther King Boulevard. No matter where you are in America, you'll find one. And you can be certain that if you're on Martin Luther King Boulevard, there's some violence going down. It isn't the safest place to be. You can't call anybody and say you're lost on MLK.

"I'm lost on Martin Luther King."

"Run! Run! Run! The media's out there!"

Sad, sad, sad!

A few states still don't celebrate MLK's birthday. Others celebrate but don't let you get off work. But federal employees get off—*including prisoners*. Even James Earl Ray, the man we convicted of killing MLK, gets the day off. Of course, he's so crazy he probably walks around prison thinking, "Hey, everybody's off today and nobody even bothered to thank me."

One way you can tell MLK's birthday is now a real holiday is that it's become a good reason for stores to have sales: furniture sales, clothing sales, white sales. They're even using his speeches in advertisements.

"I had a dream I could get an ice-cold Coca-Cola."

"Here at Bay Ridge Toyota, Toyotas are almost free . . . at last. Free at last."

MONEY MONEY MONEY MONEY

You know what racism is *really* about?

Money.

Everybody thinks the next man's got more than they do. "They got too much shit." "No, they got *all* the shit." "Wait! They got *our* shit!" White people are mad because they think they're losing everything. Blacks just think everyone else has too much shit.

> **BLACK MAN:** Y'all ain't losing shit. You all still own everything. Just go check. See?
> **WHITE MAN:** Oh, wow. You're right. We *still* own everything.

If there's one thing that scares white people more than black people, it's *poor* white people.

I've seen white people living in the projects. They've been there so long that their white friends don't even visit them anymore. You can tell because their little white kids have black nicknames, like Mookie. But it's all right when white people live in a black neighborhood. It's no big thing. We don't mind. We'll call you a name for about two days, but about the third day, you're cool. We'll give you love.

"Hey, White Bob. You want to play some ball?"

The trouble is that there are lots of broke white people now. I've seen white people so poor that they don't live in a trailer home—they live under it. The people who live *in* the trailer look down and say, "How you doing? Here's your mail." These people aren't white trash, they're white toxic waste. They're a bunch of Shaggy-looking people from *Scooby-Doo*—eating mayonnaise sandwiches, fucking their sisters, listening to John Cougar Mellencamp records.

And they're mad. They think they're broke because the black people took it all away. Not true. They're broke because they have a third-grade education and a tooth coming out of their ear. But if they see a black man who's a lawyer, they go, "How'd that nigger get that job?"

He went to school, toothy.

If people want to get their due, they have to work for it. But there are white people who think they should get theirs just because they're white.

"White? That's twenty-five thousand a year, right? At the very least. What's happened to this country?"

White people aren't used to being broke. White people go broke and it's scary. They start crying. They call the news. Next thing they're on "60 Minutes" and "20/20."

WHITE PERSON: I can't believe what's happening to us. We're Americans and we want a congressional investigation to get down to the bottom of this. My father came here on the fucking *Mayflower* and we want justice!

What do we have to do—hold a telethon for broke white people?

There's nothing scarier than a broke white man. The broker they are, the madder they are. That's when white people start forming groups and blowing up shit. Freemen. Aryan Nation. Klan. Poor, pissed-off white people are the biggest threat to the security of this country. Look at what happened in Waco, Texas. Look at the Freemen of Montana, and the Unabomber. Look at the Oklahoma City bombing. Who did it? Some broke white man so poor he had to make his bomb out of cow shit.

As a black man—as someone who's been poor—let me offer you hate group guys a few sincere words of guidance.

Things can get better. So cut out the shit!

Broke-ass white people have it bad. I'll bet you a set of black satin sheets that 80 percent of the Ku Klux Klan makes less than $13,000 a year. No wonder they hate black people, especially those who have any money. There's nothing a white guy with a penny hates more than a nigger with a nickel.

But to watch the news or read the paper, you might think

the welfare rolls are crammed only with black folks. This whole welfare controversy makes it sound like black people just don't want to work.

If I'm not mistaken, didn't black people work 200 years **for free?** They worked really hard, too. No breaks, no time off. Slaves didn't get vacations. Where could they possibly go?

> SLAVE #1: Massa gave me a vacation.
>
> SLAVE #2: Massa gave me one, too. Where you gonna go?
>
> SLAVE #1: 'Round back. Where you gonna go?
>
> SLAVE #2: To the well. You should bring your kids. It's nice over there.

Forget vacations. In all those slave movies, I'll bet you never saw a couple slaves kick back and one say to the other, "Hey, how's the cotton treating you?"

Slavery *had* an up side, though.

In the old days, even if they were poor, at least white people had slavery to make them feel exalted.

If there was one person in your life whose ass you could beat when you felt like shit, do you know how happy you would be? You could keep them locked in a room. Then, when you got frustrated, you could stick your head in and say, "Fuck you!" When you were mad, you could go in there and kick them. Horny? That's right, you could mosey in there and fuck them.

Then you could be nice to everybody else.

It was the same with segregation. It made things cool for white people. No matter how fucked up your life was, no matter how broke and dirty your house was, no matter how ignorant you were, couldn't read, couldn't count, fucking your sister, no matter how sorry and pathetic your future looked—you could rest your head on the pillow every night thinking, "I'm living better than a nigger."

White people had that.

White people lost that.

Yes, yes. Times have changed.

Segregation kept the white man in check. But black people have some money now. We have as much money as broke white people. We're coming up. Now broke black people live right next door to broke white people, and the white people don't know what the hell's going on.

They're wondering, "Oh shit. There's a lot of niggers out here? Am I becoming a nigger?"

What's really sad now is that *everybody's* broke. Black people *and* white people. Of course, black people are used to being broke.

"You broke. I'm broke. Fuck it, let's hang out."

I don't want to be broke, even though in some ways it's cool because you know who your friends are. If you're broke and someone wants to hang out with you, they *really* want to hang out with you. If you're broke and in a relationship and somebody loves you, that person *loves* you.

Anybody can love you when you're rich.

Yeah, it's tough being a white person these days.

But not that tough. I am absolutely certain.

Why? Because there's not a white person reading this book who would change places with me.

And I'm rich!

Come on. Change places with me.

See? Even you white guys making minimum wage are going, "Uh uh. I'm going to roll these white dice and ride this white thing out a *little* longer. See where it takes me."

ME: But you get a big house.

WHITE GUY: Oh, that's okay. I'll stay in my shoe box.

And that's all you need to know about the racial divide.

THE GOOD OLD DAYS

People always talk about the good old days.

When were they?

Not during Biblical times. In the Bible, there were only about three good days—just before God got around to creating the fish and animals—and the world's been fucked up since.

You think there was less crime in 1929? Maybe so. But back then, a white man could lynch a black man, rape a white woman, and get a seven-dollar fine. During Biblical times, if you did something really bad, they would rip out your tongue, tie your arms and legs to four horses, and crack them all on the ass. Or they could stone you to death. Or boil you in oil. So don't kid yourself, the world is much nicer than it once was. In fact, considering the alternatives—racks, guillotines, skinning, being fed to the lions—guns look pretty humane.

IN THE GHETTO

Before there was Compton, East St. Louis, Watts, and Harlem, there was Bed-Stuy, Brooklyn. Bedford-Stuyvesant. It's one of the original ghettos.

I grew up there.

Bed-Stuy is such a ghetto that in Billy Joel's song, "You May Be Right," he brags about walking through Bedford-Stuyvesant by himself: "I walked through a combat zone."

This strolling-through-the-ghetto feat apparently impressed white people so much that they went out and bought millions of Billy's record, earned him make-you-stupid money, and he got to fuck Christie Brinkley. All because he supposedly had the nerve to walk through my neighborhood alone.

I've walked through it alone.

How come I don't get to fuck Christie Brinkley?

I was six when my family moved to our house on Decatur Street in Bed-Stuy. We lived on the nicest block in the ghetto. Andre was four, Tony was two, and the rest of my brothers and sisters—Brian, Kenny, Andrea, and Jordan—weren't even born yet.

Some people looked down on us as "the projects people." Actually, we'd never spent a day in the projects. We'd moved to Bed-Stuy from an apartment in Crown Heights, but that didn't seem to make a difference. When we arrived, everybody wondered: "Are these gonna be the people who finally fuck up the block?"

Behind it all was their fear: "We have it *way* too nice. How long can this possibly last?"

It didn't last long.

Bed-Stuy is the kind of neighborhood where the only people with money are drug dealers; people who hit the daily number; and people who got hit by cars, sued, and got paid.

In my old neighborhood, people crossed the street real slow. And they crossed it with an attitude. "Hit me *today*, and I'll own it *tomorrow*."

I used to hate driving through Bed-Stuy in the summertime because kids would be out of school, and they'd always run into and across the street without warning. It was as if their mothers would be sitting on the stoops shouting, "Hey baby, there goes a Cadillac. Run!"

The first thing people would say when anybody got hit and lived was, "Damn, he got lucky. How'd he do it?" And they weren't referring to the fact that he lived.

One brother named Aaron had all the luck in the world. He got in two accidents in one summer and must have settled for about $40,000. Word spread quickly.

"Yo, man, Aaron just got hit by a truck."

"How the fuck does he do it? Didn't he get hit by a van last month? Boy, he's getting paid!"

Aaron could be down on the ground, blood coming out of his mouth, his leg touching his ear, and somebody would say:

"Aaron, start breathing! If you start breathing, you gonna get paid!"

Aaron is a role model for us all. I've been trying to get hit for months. I stand in the middle of Fifth Avenue for eight hours a day, disguised as a pothole. But nothing hits me.

Aaron is five minutes out of the check-cashing spot and *BLLLLLLAAAAAM!!!* He's done it again.

My mom was a ghetto snob. She didn't teach us to believe we were as good as anybody else; she raised us to believe we were *better*. When she sent me to get ribs from the Rib Shack she'd say, "Don't tell nobody where you're going." Like it was some big deal. God forbid somebody find out that a black woman in Bed-Stuy liked ribs.

My father drove a *Daily News* delivery truck. A big thing with my father was being a man. Didn't do your homework? "What kind of man you gonna be?" Running late? "What time you gotta be at work? A man gets to work on time."

ALL iN THE EXTENDED FAMiLY

My parents used to take in foster kids. It wasn't like adopting a child, where you have to provide for that kid because it's yours. It's more like babysitting for the city of New York. They actually pay you money.

We always got the foster kids in November, because my mother knew the money would help pay for our Christmas toys. One year, while this little girl, Frieda, was living with us, I got a bike. On Christmas Day, she decided to ride my bike down a flight of stairs. She didn't get hurt, but my bike got busted. I went crying to my mother.

"Ma, Frieda broke my bike."

My mother said, "I don't know why you're telling me. Frieda *bought* your bike, and she'll get you another one."

My parents never told us exactly when the kids were coming. I would just come home one day, and there'd be this kid in the yard saying, "Hey, you're my brother." And I'd say, "Who are you?"

Suddenly the house would be all crowded. We'd argue about who was gonna get in the bathroom or who drank all the Kool-Aid, or how come we'd run out of cereal.

Every year we had the same overcrowding with a different set of kids. Some came from families where there was abuse and neglect. Some were actually mentally ill. At the very least most were a little emotionally unstable. I remember one girl went to the laundry room in the middle of the night and cut the tops off all our socks.

A lot of people in our neighborhood kept foster kids. My mother was actually very good with them; she treated them like her own. But one of her friends wouldn't let her foster kids eat with her real kids. The foster children had to live in the basement. It was like apartheid in their house.

I remember one day, I went into their fridge to get some juice, and I said, "Wow, I never saw black Kool-Aid before."

My friend's mother said, "You don't want that. That's foster-kid juice."

SPARE THE ASS, SPOIL THE CHILD

People need to beat their kids. But these days parents are against hitting their children. It's the nineties and you're not supposed to do that. In one way they're right: you shouldn't smack a kid in the head or in the face.

But the ass was made for whupping. Gotta do it. Every kid needs four key ass-whippings in life, and every parent has to do their best to hand them out. They are the Stealing, Lying, Cheating, and Disrespecting ass-whippings.

Every grown-up who doesn't know how to act missed the key ass-whippings. If you can't drill it into a kid's head, you have to drill it into his butt. Please, whip your kid's ass before the government whips it for him. I feel sorry every time I see distraught parents on the news whose kid gets accused of doing something terrible. The parents say, "But my kid would never do that."

Yes, he would. But he wouldn't have if you'd have whipped his ass.

When my father wanted us to do something, we did it. If we didn't he'd wake our asses up to do it. It could have been the most meaningless thing in the world. It could have easily waited until tomorrow. But my pop would wake us up at three in the morning.

MY POP: Get up. Get up, boy. Chris, get up. It's an emergency. Get up.

ME: Is it a fire?

MY POP: No. You left the top off the ketchup.

My father also didn't want any of us to be cool.

"I noticed when you walked in here you had a little bop in your walk. No bopping around here."

Whenever I was on the phone talking to a girl, my father would make sure to mess up my cool.

I'd say, "Yeah, baby. I'll pick you up later. It ain't gonna be nobody but you and me . . ."

My father would pick up the phone: "Hey, boy, your pork and beans are ready. And tell your mom to get them drawers out the sink."

Hard to be cool with drawers in the sink.

ALL iN THE FAMiLY

Families. Weird group of people. Tough to imagine they'd get together of their own free will and say, "Let's be a family."

These days everyone's got a gay family member. It's always been that way. But today, it's more out in the open. Everyone's got at least a gay cousin. You knew he was gay when you were a kid. You played ball. He jumped rope. But he's your cousin and you loved him.

I've got a gay uncle.

We call him Aunt Tom.

I love my Aunt Tom. I know that if I was in a fight, Aunt Tom would take off his pumps and whip some ass. I love my gay uncle. But the rest of the family won't admit he's gay. They say, "No, he's just slow."

Just slow?

Fifty-five years old and never had a woman? Always has his 18-year-old "friend" over?

"This is my friend from work."

Aunt Tom's preference is obvious, but my other uncles keep coming up with these weird schemes to find out if he's gay or not.

"Okay. We're going to invite him over, right, and we're going to have some strippers acting like plumbers. They'll fix the pipes but wear miniskirts with nothing on under 'em. And when they bend over to fix the pipes, if he don't look—he's a faggot."

I love my gay uncle.

I love him more than my stealing uncle.

My Uncle Byron steals shit from the house all the time. He's been doing it for twenty years. He steals little shit. Candle holders. Ashtrays. It's gotten so that we just leave things out for him.

"Should we throw that away?"

"No, leave it out. Let Byron steal it."

Uncle Byron takes stuff all the time—but only shit he thinks you would never, ever notice. Like spoons. He took all the spoons. Now I'm eating Cheerios with a fork. But when that happens, you don't think somebody *stole* them. You just think they fell behind something. You blame yourself.

Uncle Byron also steals pillowcases. What kind of tired, ignorant shit is that? What asshole steals your pillowcases? When you look around and all your pillowcases are gone, you don't think somebody stole them. You're not calling the cops over pillowcases. You think maybe they got lost in the dryer. They'll turn up.

One day I went over to his house and saw all my shit. My sheets were his curtains. And he had the nerve to say, "Make yourself at home."

Then you have your fucked-up cousins; the ones your mother wouldn't let you hang out with when you were a kid. They grow up and you see why. Momma was right. I have a cousin in jail. Shot a cop. **Shot a cop!** Went to jail. Got out. You know the justice system's fucked up when they let your family out early, and you say, "Hey, wait a minute, this is a little too soon." When I saw my cousin at my doorstep I said, "How the fuck did you get out?" It scared me to see him. I tried to make it to the phone quickly, just to let someone know he was over. I had to whisper.

"Hey, what's up, Joe? I just want you to know Bob's here. We're just chillin'. Having fun."

Of course, that's the code for: "I want you know that if I'm dead, he did it."

UNCLE MiKEY

Every family also has a relative like Uncle Mikey. Mikey is crazy. Black people, as a rule, *aren't* crazy, but some black people slip through the cracks and there's nothing we can do to help ourselves.

Mikey was definitely crazy. I know because all I had to do was ask him, "What time is it?"

He'd look at his watch, look at me, and then he'd say, "If you want to feel funky, feel free. But pulleeeze don't spread that funk on me."

Because Uncle Mikey was crazy, he also thought he was funny.

Everybody knows somebody who's funny at the water cooler or around the dinner table. Unfortunately, lots of those people also think they can easily do stand-up. And people believe them. Somehow, in this crazy culture, "funny guy" and "professional comedian" have ended up meaning the same thing.

Uncle Mikey is *not* a professional comedian. But don't try to tell him that. He thinks he's ready to do "The Tonight Show" with Jay Leno.

LENO: Ladies and gentlemen, our first guest is a security guard for Popeye's Fried Chicken. You don't know him, you don't love him, but give him a big welcome anyway. Mikey!

                         (Mikey strolls out, kisses guest Penny Marshall, shakes hands with Jay, takes a seat.)

                         So Mikey, what have you been doing?

UNCLE MIKEY: You know, Jay, just trying to stop people from stealing chicken. Actually, *I* don't stop them from stealing. Popeye's got that thick, bullet-proof Plexiglas. That's what really stops them. The glass is post-office thick. If a motherfucker can get through there, I'm going to have to run.

LENO: Now, when you guard the chicken, Mikey, do they give you a gun?

UNCLE MIKEY: Naw, man. Do you believe that shit? I guess

	they scared I'ma rob the stuff. If they paid me a little more, they wouldn't have nothing to worry about. Cheap motherfuckers.
LENO:	Uh, Mikey could you just stop cursing?
UNCLE MIKEY:	What you mean, cursing? Ain't no chil'ren here. We grown people. We grown. Kevin Eubanks, you grown, right? Penny Marshall, you grown, right?
PENNY MARSHALL:	Right.
UNCLE MIKEY:	Penny Marshall, you know I always did love you. Ever since you was on "Laverne and Shirley." Me and my boys would watch the show and say, "Which one would you fuck?" And I always picked you.
PENNY MARSHALL:	Thank you, I think.
UNCLE MIKEY:	Penny, I don't know what you're doing after the show but I know a great little chicken shack we could go to. By the way, you know who got a big ass, Jay? Debbie Allen got a big ass.
LENO:	Mikey, please stop cursing.
UNCLE MIKEY:	What you mean, stop cursing? You can curse on TV now. I was watching "Def Comedy Jam" the other night and Doodoo Man was cursing his ass off.
LENO:	Mikey, that wasn't TV, that was HBO.
UNCLE MIKEY:	HBO, NBO, C-3PO, it's all the same.
LENO:	(sliding Mikey a mug) Why don't you drink some water and calm down.
UNCLE MIKEY:	Do I look like a plant? You better get me some Colt .45 before I drop-kick you in the chin.
LENO:	(smirks, shrugs apologetically to the audience) We'll be right back after this commercial.
UNCLE MIKEY:	Right back? Where the fuck we going?

THE DiRT ROAD NOT TAKEN

So much of a person's life is determined by geography. I was actually born in Andrews, South Carolina, but moving to New York had a dramatic influence on me. If I had stayed in South Carolina, not only would I not have become a comedian, but my whole life would have turned out differently:

Feb. 7, 1966, 10 a.m.: Rose Rock gives birth to what she thinks is a boy, and names him Chris. Later that same day, Rose Rock goes back to her job as wipe-up girl at Rico's Hog Slaughtering Factory. Rico congratulates Rose and gives her a free bag of snouts.

July 20, 1971, age 5: Chris takes first step. (Life really is slower in the South.) The next day, good news and bad news. Good news: Chris takes his second step. Bad news: It's off a dock, and he's almost eaten by killer catfish.

April 3, 1973, age 7: Chris utters his first words: "No one makes a better rum cake than Haile Selassie."

October 31, 1974, age 8: Chris goes to the Halloween Ball and wins 200 dollars' worth of boiled peanuts as first prize for his Grits Man get-up. He's happy, but it takes him two months to get the costume out of his hair.

September 12, 1981, age 15: After much deliberation, Chris elects to continue his education and enters fourth grade.

March 4, 1983, age 17: Chris loses his virginity to an albino goat. Later, Chris is embarrassed: he discovers the goat lied to him, claiming only to be "light-skinned."

June 27, 1985, age 19: Chris spends a night in the hoosegow after getting into a brawl at a Charlie Pride concert.

August 14, 1990, age 24: Chris gets a job installing hand blowers in outhouses, a career with a promising future.

January 13, 1992, age 25: Chris enters a talent show as a comedian, but loses to his Uncle Mikey.

THE LiTTLE GUY—
AND OTHER
LiFE SHAPiNG EXPERiENCES

I've always been a little guy. This can be a problem. Your height and weight really determine how rough your childhood's going to be.

On my first day of junior high school, some kids got robbed. But I got special treatment. A guy turned me upside down and shook the money out of my pockets. That's what happens when you're little. A normal-sized guy would at least get the respect of being punched in the face before he got robbed.

Now that I'm a man, I'm average height, but I weigh less than 150 pounds. So I still have problems. If I step on another man's shoes and say I'm sorry, I might get yelled at and even end up in a fight. If I weighed 175 pounds, the apology would be accepted without question. I can speak to a cute girl at a party, but if her man shows up and he's big, I'm in line for an ass-whipping.

Life is full of limitations. For instance, when you're a little guy you have to avoid going out with women who like to make trouble. Little Miss Instigation. She'll start shit like she's ready to whup some ass—without thinking about what might happen to you. Like the time I took a date to the movies and someone was smoking.

> HER: Will you put that out!
> ME: Are you trying to get us killed? Are you? Don't you know the rules? If you're going to say some shit you have to be prepared to do some shit. Or else, shut up!

But she didn't listen. Later, there were some people talking:

> HER: Would you shut up!

ME: Honey, what is wrong with you? Are *you* gonna fight? Then
      be quiet.

Then someone stepped on her foot.

HER: You can at least say excuse me!
ME: Let it go. Let it slide. Is the shoe broken?
BIG GUY: Yeah. Shut up, bitch.
HER: He called me a bitch!
ME: Well, were you acting bitchy? He didn't call me a bitch.
          I'm not gonna get my ass whupped over this shit. I just
          met you. I barely know you!

Big or little, just remember: you can't get your ass whupped
in front of a woman you know. You just can't. We act like we're
civilized people and say relationships are about the inner person, but it's bullshit. If you get your ass whupped in front of a
woman, that's the end of the relationship. It is over!

A woman can't be around any man who doesn't make her
feel safe. She's got to feel protected. If guns are going off, she's
got to be thinking, "It's okay. I'm with my man." She can't be
with a man who's scared.

Sometimes this can be confusing.

If there's going to be a fight, the woman will act like she
doesn't want you to fight.

"No, no, no! No, no! We're going to go! No, I don't want
you to fight. Don't fight."

But if you do, and you whup somebody's ass, your woman
will tell that story for ten years.

Martin Luther King was a little guy. Malcolm X was a big guy.
The little guy talked about us all getting along. The big guy
talked about whupping ass. It wasn't an accident.

I know MLK was a devout Christian and humanitarian, but
don't think for a minute that his physical being didn't affect his

approach to problem solving. If he was four or five inches taller and had a little bit more muscle on him, his message might have been totally different.

We might all be dead right now.

Gandhi was a little guy. Farrakhan is a big guy.

Big guys always think they can win. Little guys know what can happen. Little guys understand an ass-whipping. Little guys only fight when there's no other choice.

SCHOOL DAZE

Hand-in-hand with my size, the experience that probably shaped my life most was being bused to school starting when I was seven years old.

It wasn't only me. Black kids in New York City and around the country got bused. That's what time it was in America. All of us were supposedly heading off to a better education. A lot of people looked at busing as this great thing:

"Ooh, we get to go to *white* schools."

I got bused from Bed-Stuy to a white school in a poor white neighborhood: Gerretson Beach, Brooklyn. It was even worse than where I lived. My parents assumed I'd get a better education in a better neighborhood. What I actually got was a worse education in a worse neighborhood. And a whole bunch of ass-whippings.

Nobody was glad to see me.

Busing's tough. I had to get up every morning at 6:00 a.m. to go to school to compete with white kids who didn't have to wake up until 8:00 a.m.

That's not fair.

One teacher said, "Oh, Chris can't read."

I thought, "No. Chris is fucking tired."

It was also hard being the only black kid in my class.

Whenever they would do that lesson on slavery, everyone would turn around and look at me.

Talk about your fucking stereotypes!

(And sometimes a teacher would come to me when she was in a particular jam after school: "Mr. Rock, it appears I have locked my keys in my car. Could you help me get them out?")

Everybody knew my name. Most kids want to be popular. But not that kind of popular. I felt like Franklin in the "Peanuts" comic strip.

I've watched those "Peanuts" specials for twenty-something years, and they never let Franklin say anything. Every other character had an identifiable trait. Charlie was awkward. Lucy was a bitch. Linus was co-dependent. Schroeder loved music. Peppermint Patty was a lesbian. That's right, Peppermint Patty was a lesbian. (I'm sure if you could ask her what her favorite song is, she'd say "Constant Craving.") Anyway, they never gave Franklin anything to say.

Come on, Charles Schulz, help us out here. Give him something. Maybe a Jamaican accent.

"Hey, Charlie Brown, mon, le's go get some curry goat."

You know what's really sad, they didn't invite Franklin to any of the parties. They invited the dog, though. Snoopy would be dancing his ass off. But Franklin was barred.

This is the guy I related to. Of course, Franklin had the good fortune to be in a cartoon.

This was my real life.

Guys were always hitting me. Everybody called me nigger. The guys would put a lot of stank in it, like "Ya fuckin' nigger." The girls would be nice. They would say, "Hi, Nigger," like it was a nickname. It caused some mild psychological damage. I couldn't tie my shoes until I was 9, I wet the bed until I was 13, and I still can't go to sleep without Mommy making sure the Boogie Man isn't under the bed.

Kids are the cruelest, meanest, nastiest people on Earth. Don't put anything past them. When the Pan Am jet blew up, people were talking about terrorists. I said, "Those fucking kids."

Nobody knows who killed Kennedy.

I say, ask a kid.

A DiFFERENT KiND OF HiGH SCHOOL REUNiON

Fifteen years later, I got off a plane coming back from L.A. and my limo driver was a white guy who used to spit in my face at school. When you bump into someone who used to kick your ass, for a moment you feel that same fear. Fear is the same whether you're 7 years old or 30. But he talked like we were best friends. He said he told everybody he went to school with me, but nobody believed him. Meanwhile, I'm thinking, "Why don't you show them the eye you kicked out of my head?"

I was uncomfortable for the whole ride.

When we got back to my house I made sure to give him a big tip. I knew it would mess with his mind.

Why? On "Bugs Bunny," when would Elmer Fudd get the maddest? When Bugs shot him in the face? No. When Bugs dropped an anvil on his head? No. It was when Bugs kissed him. So my tip was like a kiss. I also figured that if I didn't give him a big tip, that in his mind it would validate all the times he kicked my ass.

Just as I was about to go inside, he made his move. He wanted to take our new relationship a step further. He gave me his card and said we should hang out sometime.

I was ready to curse him out and say, "Why would I ever want to hang out with you?"

That's when another cartoon popped into my head. It was an old episode of "Bugs Bunny and Friends." The one with

Sam the sheepdog and Ralph the wolf. Sam's job was to guard the sheep from Ralph, and this usually resulted in Fred getting the shit beaten out of him. But at the end of the day, the whistle would blow, and the two of them would pull out a time card, punch the clock, and say, "See ya tomorrow."

That's when I realized that this guy and I had just been playing our roles. He was a white boy. I was some nigger in an all-white school. It was his job to treat me like shit.

Okay. No hard feelings.

FLOAT ON

Can't deal with responsibility? Feel like a failure?

There's hope.

Dope and liquor are like "happy" in a bottle. They're the ultimate escape from reality. You get to float; everybody else has to walk.

The first high is always the best high. After that, you're just trying to get back to the original feeling. The first high is like home. I mean home-home. Your mother's womb.

You're in warm water, just sloshing around. You don't even have a name yet. You don't need one. You've got shelter, you've got food, and everything you do is okay.

To top it off, you won't have to pay a bill for another 20 years.

HOW iT ALL GETS STARTED

People against drugs say it all starts with beer.

> **ADDICT:** "Ahh man, I'm hitting the pipe. Can't fuck with that beer no more."

I once saw my father drink nine beers in a row while he was driving. It seemed to have no effect. But the fact that he drank nine beers told me that he was addicted on some level. Unless you're Spuds MacKenzie, you don't drink nine beers because you're thirsty.

You wouldn't drink nine glasses of Kool-Aid.

Actually, I think all addiction starts with soda. Every drunkie and junkie did soda first. But no one counts that. Maybe they should. The soda connection is clear. Why isn't a presidential commission looking into this? Or at least some guys from the National Carbonation Council.

Okay, okay. Getting hooked on drugs is no joke. Some people lose everything. But you know what? I only feel sorry for the *original* alcoholics and drug addicts. They had no idea what they were getting into. They were just trying something different and got caught up.

But if you've seen a couple generations destroy themselves, and then *you* start getting high, *you're* an asshole.

I don't get high, but sometimes I wish I did. That way, when I messed up in life I would have an excuse. But right now there's no rehab for stupidity. So I don't do it. I've seen it ruin too many lives—like about 80 percent of the people I grew up with.

PLASTIC JONES

Everybody's addicted to something. It's not always alcohol, cigarettes, or crack. Some people are addicted to popping the bubbles in bubble wrap.

I know. I had a bad case of it for a while. I would constantly open other people's packages and pinch the protective plastic. When I couldn't get my hands on bubble wrap, I would pop cleaner bags and Hefty bags and Twinkies packages. It got to a point where it was all I did all day. People tried to help me, but I wouldn't listen.

I lost my job, I lost my friends, I lost my woman.

Then one day my habit almost got me killed. I intentionally crashed my car into a tree so I could pop the air bag. Now I realize that was the luckiest day of my life. I'd finally hit rock bottom. I spent four months in the hospital, with massive head wounds, and was forced to quit cold turkey. It wasn't easy. I kept wanting to pop the I.V. bag, but the doctors were hip and tied me to the bed.

Now, my life is slowly coming back together. I let my woman open everything. When we send gifts we pack them with those foam "peanuts" that know how to run away when you try to sweep them up. Last week I went to a Key Food Supermarket grand opening and never even touched the balloons.

I wanted to.

Didn't.

But I still have my tough moments. Every now and then, whenever I see a UPS truck, I almost have an orgasm.

JUST SAID NO

I've smoked pot twice.

It was peer pressure, I swear.

The first time nothing happened. The second time, I was at a party—one of those wild affairs right out of *Less Than Zero*, only no guys had their heads buried in other guys' laps. I was lying on a bed thinking, "Shit, what the fuck did she put in the pipe? Now I know why people do this!"

I was so high I found the host and said, "Oh man, you got to fix your house. It's tilted! The earthquake really fucked up your house, man."

It took me a few seconds to realize that only I was tilted. That's when I stopped getting high.

But my brother gets high. However, he doesn't eat pork. He says pork's no good for you. That's right. Would you believe that there are also people who will shoot heroin but won't eat red meat? They say, "Red meat? That'll kill you." Well, yes, if you put it in a needle and shoot it into your arm. Just the size of the needle will kill you.

Some folks figure because they go to work every day, they're not really addicts. I have friends in their late 30s who make $60,000 a year in jobs like construction and plumbing. They have it together just enough to get to and from work, hustle up some dinner in the evenings, and buy a suit on Easter. They live at home and spend $5,000 on necessities and the other $55,000 getting high.

It's true. You *can* spend $55,000 getting high. No matter how much money you make, you can easily fit it into a crack pipe.

*   *   *

I don't drink, either.

Wherever people drink there's always an altercation.

I don't drink because I can't fight.

I read instead. Not only does it help me escape everyday pressures, but I've never seen a fight in the library. You never hear somebody yelling, "Matthew! Put . . . the . . . book . . . down!"

"At least let me flip this page."

"No. You've had a little too much to read. You're going to have to leave now."

AN OFFER YOU CAN'T REFUSE

Everyone's mad at drug dealers. They say dealers force drugs on people. They don't force drugs. They don't have to.

A drug dealer is not like a door-to-door encyclopedia or vacuum cleaner salesperson. You won't hear a pusher saying, "Man, oh man, how am I gonna get rid of all this crack? It's just piled up in my house. Kid's got nowhere to sleep. Even the roaches are moving out, looking for a place with an extra bedroom."

Dealers *offer* drugs.

I'm 31 years old and nobody's ever forced anything on me. If a dealer says, "Hey man, you want some smack?" and I say, "No," that's it. How many of you have been on your way to a piano recital, got some heroin forced on your ass, and found yourself in an alley shooting up?

Just like I thought. Only a few.

Drug dealers only offer, but Jehovah's Witnesses will break a fucking toe trying to get in your house to read you a copy of *The Watchtower*.

I always try to be nice.

First, I say I'm on the phone and can't talk now. If they don't leave, I say I'm on the phone with God and I don't think I ought to keep Him waiting. If they still don't leave, I tell them I was just going to the bathroom to shoot up and there's no way anyone who wants to read to me from a comic book about God is going to keep me from my drugs—which, by the way, I willingly bought. But if they insist on coming in, they can at least help tie me off.

That usually does it.

Actually, I have no problem with the Jehovah's Witnesses. In fact, I'm all for freedom of religion.

But do they always have to get up so early?

One morning I heard my bell ring at dawn. I figured it was the UPS man with a package. I busted my ass down the stairs, trembling, because I couldn't wait to get my hands on that bubble wrap. Next thing I knew I was stuck at the door, sand in my eyes, wearing my pj's with the feet, talking to some Jehovah's Witnesses. (They always travel in pairs. They know it's harder to pick off two moving targets than one wandering around on his or her own.)

ME: It's six o'clock in the morning. Are you crazy?

WITNESS: God is *always* up. God is *always* watching you.

ME: Yeah, well, God and everybody else might actually be able to get some sleep if you'd stayed in bed this morning. Isn't there something somewhere about resting on the seventh day?

THEM: So you know your Scripture.

Then they just smiled that patient smile—and gave me the Big News!

WITNESS: Did you know that Jesus was black?

ME: No kidding? (I said this in a way that let them know I'm not easily impressed.)

They didn't react. Then the one in the shiny blue suit started reading from the literature: "He had hair like a lamb, skin of bronze and he averaged thirty-three points a game."

ME: No shit? Musta had some move to the basket. Say, why don't y'all come on in? I'll put on some coffee and wake my wife.

SOME THiNGS i KNOW ABOUT CRACK

- It makes girls fuck guys they'd never be caught dead fucking.

- If you're an asshole, it makes you a bigger asshole.

- It helps you lose weight.

When cocaine got too expensive for the 'hood, crack was invented. Now brothers with fourth-grade educations go down into their basements and become mad scientists. These guys don't know shit about chemistry. They think a periodic table is something their old ladies get at the doctor so they can tell when they might get pregnant.

But they know how to make some crack.

Remember when you were in school and they said you had to learn the metric system because it's the future? Today the only people you hear talking about grams and kilos are drug dealers—not the kind of folks you think of as having a future.

* * *

Crack is everywhere. People say it's destroying the black community. They say it's destroying the ghetto. Like the ghetto was so nice *before* crack? Like everyone in the 'hood had a mansion, a yacht, and a swimming pool, then crack came by and dried it all up.

But why always focus on the negative? What about the good side of crack?

If you're up at the right hour you can get a VCR for $1.50. You can furnish your whole house for $10.95. Why? Because of crack.

Crack makes Christmas gift-buying easy. You drive up in a new car. You tell your wife, "I love you so much. This is yours." She just stares at you and says, "Ooh, you *shouldn't* have." And you know what? You didn't. You just bought it from a crackhead for five dollars.

Crack is so addictive that if the new way to get high was to put it on a bullet, shoot it through a gun, and take a lick as it came out of the barrel, crackheads would try it. You'd see two guys, one holding the gun and the other with his tongue out.

CRACKHEAD #1: You ready to get high, muthafucker?
CRACKHEAD #2: Hhhnnnuunnnhh?
CRACKHEAD #1: I said, "You ready?"
CRACKHEAD #2: Uhhunnnh.

BANG!

A second later, Crackhead #1 stares stupidly down at his friend on the ground. He's bloody. He's not moving. He pokes him with his big toe.

Nothing.

Oh shit. Crackhead #1 feels a scream welling up inside. He can't hold on any more. He lets it out.

"Muthafucker! Get up. Get up. You gotta do *me!*"

A DAY iN THE LiFE OF A FUNCTiONAL DRUG ADDiCT

7 a.m. He gets up sluggish, showers, and then picks something to wear from the four items of clothing he still owns. (Can't be blowing money on clothes.)

8:15 a.m. Arrives at work fifteen minutes late for the 60th time this year. He doesn't even bother with an excuse. Instead, he tries to look insanely busy and gets a few things done.

Lunch: Sucks down a tall can of St. Ides malt liquor and a pack of chocolate donuts. Chases the scent of alcohol with a stick of gum. Can't spend too much money because it'll cut into his stash for drugs. Has to choose "meals" that'll fill him up.

5 p.m. He hops the subway turnstile to head home. (Saving a buck-fifty a ride adds up when you need drugs.)

5:45 p.m. He arrives in the neighborhood and immediately goes to the corner to hang out with the *non*functioning drug addicts. Waits for the other functioning drug addicts to get home.

6:30 p.m. Finally, the gang's all there and someone says, "Who's buying the beer?" They get a couple of six packs and stand around on the corner getting lit and talking about their big plans:

    One is going to buy a car.

    Another one's looking at a house.

    Somebody's talking about a trip to Jamaica.

    One is getting tickets to a Knicks game.

    Another mentions his mutual fund investments.

To a stranger walking by, the whole conversation sounds perfectly normal. But to anyone who knows them, it's all bull-shit. They've been saying this same shit for 16 years.

8:30 p.m. Time to go home. He turns the key in the door, opens it, and says hello to his mother. She's not living there because she's old and sick and he's taking care of her. She's there be-cause *he* lives with *her*. And though he tells his friends he pays rent, he hasn't given her a dime in years. He doesn't steal, much, and he's not violent, so she tolerates his trifling ass.

9:08 p.m. He hears his mother call. Kelly, one of his girlfriends, is on the phone. He's 38 and she's 17—and not a smart 17. Why would a 38-year-old be with a dense 17-year-old? Because only a young, dumb girl would go for his shit. Only a 17-year-old would be impressed by the concept of a person having his own room. They talk and he finally says, "I'll see you later," and hangs up. That's code for: "Come over here right now and knock on the side door." That way his mother won't hear.

9:25 p.m. He and Kelly share the second joint of the night. He makes a futile attempt to have a conversation, but since they have nothing in common, they just fuck.

10:15 p.m. After sex, she starts telling him how he never takes her anyplace.
"When are we going out to dinner?" she asks.
"Right now," he says. Then they walk over to the corner Chinese take-out with the bullet-proof glass. "Gimme the usual," he says.

10:33 p.m. As they're walking out of the Chinese spot, his get-high buddy Craig walks up and says to Kelly, "Can you excuse us for a second?" He talks to Craig for about four minutes and then says to Kelly, "Me and Craig have to take care of some business."

He reaches inside the bag, grabs the beer and a chicken wing, gives her the box with the wings and pork-fried rice, and promises to catch up with her later.

"By the way," he says, "do you have ten dollars I can borrow? I'll pay you back tomorrow."

"But I paid for the food and I gave you ten dollars yesterday," she says.

He says, "Shut up and give me the money."

She digs in her pocket and hands him two five-dollar bills.

10:40 p.m. He and Craig go see Darius, the drug dealer. They've got money for about twenty dollars' worth of crack. Why twenty dollars? Because he's only going to do a little bit, so he can go to sleep early and be ready for work tomorrow.

10:53 p.m. He and Craig go to Craig's and enter through the side door. Craig also lives with his mother. In the basement, they light incense to cover the smell, and then fire up the pipe.

Midnight: For some weird reason he's not *that* tired. He says, "What the heck, let's get high some more."

He figures that as long as he gets six hours of sleep, it's okay. So he goes by the money machine, takes out the cash he'd set aside for his child-support payment, and then doubles back to his drug-dealer friend.

1:15 a.m. They've smoked it all and now it's time to leave Craig's house. He's determined he's *not* going to get high again. Can't. Doesn't have the money, and besides, he needs the sleep. So he goes home, and when he gets there, he sees a woman with a familiar face, sitting on his stoop. It's Pat, his crackhead girlfriend.

Back in high school, when she was the prom queen and

all-around big woman on campus, she wouldn't give him the time of day. Now she's a crackhead and they're close—which means she'll blow him for the prize in a Cracker Jack box if she thinks she can sell it for more drugs.

She says, "I was by Darius's house, and he said y'all just left. You got any get-high?"

And right then, he remembers the vial in his pocket that he hid from Craig.

1:48 a.m. They sneak into his mother's house and he and Pat tip-toe up to his room and get high. Afterward, they make a futile attempt at conversation. But aside from crack, they have nothing in common, so they just have sex. The fact that she sleeps with various men—without a condom—to obtain crack, does not deter him from having sex with her, also without a condom. Somehow he still believes that 99 percent of the people who get AIDS are gay. The other one percent are lying fags.

2:20 a.m. He still wants to get high. And he figures, "Hey, if I get four hours' sleep, I'll be okay." But he has no money, except $1.50, which he may or may not use to get on the train tomorrow. So he starts looking around his mother's house for things to sell to Darius. He tries to take things she won't notice, like one speaker. She won't think the speaker's gone, she'll think the balance is off on the system. He takes all the forks out of her silver set. She can eat chicken cutlet with a spoon. He even grabs the half pound of ground beef she was thawing in the sink for spaghetti sauce. After all, it's for her own good. Red meat will kill you.

At Darius's, he discovers he has half the money he needs. So for the next hour and a half, he becomes a crack pimp while Pam, his crackhead girlfriend, turns a few tricks. Then they go back to Darius's house, get more crack, and go back to his mother's and smoke it up.

Another futile attempt at small talk, then more unprotected

sex. Then he tells her to go, because soon it will be daylight and he doesn't want anybody to know he's fucking a crack-head. See, *he* likes to smoke crack; *she's* a crackhead. There's a difference.

She leaves because she's a drifting crack whore and she literally sleeps where she ends up.

4:30 a.m. He figures he'll be OK as long as he gets three hours of sleep. But then there's a knock on the side door. It's Kelly. She says she couldn't sleep, and now he suspects *she* may be a crackhead. But he lets her in anyway, and the two of them fall into a stupor. When the alarm wakes him at seven, he stumbles into the bathroom, takes a half-assed shower, and gets dressed. Then he sends Kelly off to high school and heads out himself for another hard day repairing the foundation of the Brooklyn Bridge.

A MODEST PROPOSAL

People say we should just legalize drugs and deal with it.

Let me clue you in.

The only reason drugs *aren't* legal is because white guys didn't think of making cocaine first. If drugs were made in America by white guys, they would have been legal twenty years ago—when we could have enjoyed them.

Should we legalize drugs? I don't know. Imagine America a year after drugs are cool. There'd be drug sales everywhere. You could buy them at Macy's, or Price Club, or Pathmark—just like alcohol, tobacco, and gum. The Macy's TV ad would be, "This week Macy's got crack! You think JC Penney's got crack? We got *crack*! And with every $35 purchase of Estée

Lauder products, a dime bag of crack in its own designer vial, suitable for reuse again and again."

But then we'd also have guys like Jesse Jackson mad because black people aren't buying crack in the black community.

"Buy your crack from a black crack dealer, keep it in the 'hood."

Another reason we should legalize drugs is so that my functional-drug-addict friends' mothers could have something to brag about.

"You know Ronald has his own crack house now. I drive by it every day. Ronald even got his own crackheads, and sometimes they come by and clean up my house. Sometimes they clean *out* my house, but my son buys me new stuff, so it don't matter."

Instead, we're having a war on drugs.

Just what is a *war* on drugs?

Sounds like a bunch of soldiers in a field shooting at five-pound bags of weed. A war on drugs makes as much sense as a war on cucumbers. No cucumber is going to hurt you unless you eat it, and even then the worst it might do is give you a little gas.

The problem is not the drugs. It's the behavior that goes with drugs. And the violence. A lot of people are hurt or killed while drug dealers are fighting over territory and money. If you take that away, then most of the damage drugs do is to the individuals who choose to use.

Do we need a whole war on drugs to protect assholes? We should know better. Everything that happened with crack happened before with alcohol. You had gang wars. You had bootleggers making windfall profits. There were even drive-by shootings.

The drive-by is not a new concept, you know. The cowboys had ride-bys. They'd ride-by and shoot up a whole town.

Maybe it was a gallop-by. In the Cro-Magnon days they had walk-bys. You steal the magic berries a caveman chewed to get high, and he'd walk-by and club your ass.

Even though we're at war against drugs, I'm not sure we really want to win. Some of our most moral leaders don't want to get rid of drugs because, in their own sick way, they think drugs are good for the economy. They're right. Drugs help get more people in jail. Then corrections officers can sell inmates drugs to help them pass the time. I know, I know. It's corrupt. But sometimes you just need two jobs to make ends meet.

Our authority figures love drugs. Somewhere, there's a corrections officer sitting down to dinner, saying, "Thank God for this food, the love we share, and the cocaine traffic into south Florida."

THE WAGES OF SIN

Why do famous people die of drug overdoses when they have everything in the world anyone could want?

Because they have everything in the world anyone could want. And then they want more of it. And when that doesn't make them happy, they get high, which also doesn't make them happy, so they get higher—and then next thing you know they get dead.

When you've got a lot of money—especially if you're young—you feel invincible. A pocket full of money and boredom are sinning's best friends. You'll try anything.

Famous people O.D. because they can get their hands on too much stuff. John Belushi is not dead because he was addicted to cocaine. He's dead because he could get his hands on 100 grams. If he had made four dollars an hour, he'd be alive today.

Richard Pryor blew himself up. If he was poor, he probably only would have burnt a cuff.

THE SEX OF iT

I know guys who normally would never think of doing crack, yet they're hooked on it because it's so easy to fuck crack girls. They don't need crack. They need a fucking psychiatrist. They do it because they can't handle sex with a real woman. Too many unpredictable elements. You have to be able to compromise. You have to be able to hold a conversation. You have to be able to think about more than just crack and how to get the money to buy more crack.

If you catch the crack girl early on she can still look fine. Three weeks into the addiction, no one can tell the difference— except that a girl who would normally never talk to you, a girl you'd put on a fucking pedestal, will fuck you for five or ten dollars.

PEOPLE ARE ALWAYS GOiNG TO GET HiGH

Drugs, drugs, drugs. No matter what anyone says or does, the truth is that drugs have been around from the beginning—and they'll be here at the end.

Why? Because people like to get high.

You could get rid of all the illegal drugs in the world. It wouldn't change a thing. People will just think of new ways to get toasted.

"Check this out. Check this out. You get a baby's bottle, right? Fill it up with high-test gasoline and a week-old lima bean. Let it sit overnight. Suck it all down. Man, you'll get fucked up!"

Some people *live* to get high. They're thinking about getting high right now. They're saying, "Damn, how many more pages in this book? No way. I can't wait that long. Soon as I finish this sentence, I'm gonna get high."

CASH FLOW

When I was a kid, my mother would never give money to a white bum. She'd take one look at him and say, "No reason for that."

As I got older, I began to understand.

In this country, being white is like having five dollars; being black is like being fifty cents short.

OH, TO BE RICH AND BLACK

Black people are the brokest people on earth. Still, every now and then you see a black person with a lot of money. But it's not like they represent everybody. Or anybody.

Yeah, Oprah's rich. She makes hundreds of millions a year. That's really great. But if Bill Gates woke up with Oprah's money, he'd jump out the fucking window. He'd shoot his kids in the head. No way he wants to be *that* poor.

Shaquille O'Neal also has lots of money. But a white man wrote the check.

"Here you go, Shaq. Buy yourself a bouncing car or something."

Ever see the list of the richest people in the country? They're always obscure white guys like Jackie Allen, the billionaire tycoon who invented napkins. Or Lance Mays, the gumball heir. These guys are so rich that Donald Trump isn't even on the list.

Ever see a list of the richest *black* people in the country? Oprah's on there. Cosby. Michael Jordan. Magic Johnson. Tiger Woods. Movie stars. But you can't get past number eight without running across a brother who just hit the Lotto jackpot last week.

A lot of rich people used to be nerds. They were smart, but they were ugly. They didn't get the girl. They got chosen last for sports. And TV perpetuated the stereotype. Go ahead. Name three very smart, but also popular, good-looking kids on TV. Didn't think you could.

I'd like to see real former nerds do public service announcements showing how much fun they're having right now.

"Hi. I'm Bill Gates. When I was eight, someone shook me upside-down and took the money out of my pockets. When I was a teenager, I never got laid. I was smart and nice, but I had to keep to myself.

"Today I'm a billionaire."

People ask me for money all the time. In fact, they ask me for money the way they ask other people for the *time*. Someone always wants to know if I can help them buy a car or a house. They act like I won the lottery and have a spare five million.

And they have no intention of ever paying it back because no one thinks a celebrity works for it. People don't look at show business as a job. They think it's the ultimate get-over. The ultimate "you got lucky." This is especially true if you're a comedian because everybody knows somebody who's funny— *and who they know is funnier than you.*

When you're in show business, people think you're making twice as much money as you are. For my one scene in *Beverly Hills Cop II*, I earned $600. For *New Jack City*, I made $11,000. That's not bad for a few weeks' work, but if you stretch it out over a year, you're not talking about much. My first year of "Saturday Night Live," I made $90,000. After taxes, that's about $50,000. Then I paid my agent ten percent, my manager 15 percent, and my lawyer five percent. That left me with $36,000. That year, my brother Andre made more than that.

Maybe I should have given my friends Andre's number.

BiG TROUBLE WiTH MONEY

Black folks have trouble with money. White folks can handle money because they've had it a lot longer than we have. White people know to take enough money with them when they go out of the house. "Fifteen dollars? No problem. Here's a twenty."

Brothers always struggle at the cash register.

"Fifteen dollars? You sure? You positive? Can you ring that up again? All right, put back the Kit Kat bar."

A brother will buy a pair of shades for $300—knowing good and well his rent is $350.

What kind of ignorant shit is that?

White people believe in banks. Not black people. If a

brother hits the Lotto for ten million, he'll keep nine million in his pocket.

"You got change for a hundred thou?"

A white man gets rich and he puts his money in the bank. His money makes more money for him. A black man gets rich and it's just the countdown to him being broke.

When white people die they leave a will. If a brother dies he leaves a bill.

White people are good with their credit cards. White people use their credit cards with confidence.

"Put it on my card!"

Ever see a black woman use her credit card? It's one of the saddest sights in the whole world. Her hands are shaking as she pulls out the plastic. And while the clerk rings up the sale, what's the black woman doing? Crossing her fingers. Praying.

"Oh, Lord, please let it go through. Don't embarrass me in here today, Lord. Please Lord. I only got a thirteen-dollar limit. Lord, Lord, Lord. Please let it go through."

Of course, they always embarrass her.

"Declined."

"What?"

"Declined."

And she'll try to play it off.

"Who is Devine? Anybody seen Devine?"

"No, declined. You. Lady with the red weave. **Declined!**"

Right at that moment she figures it can't get any worse.

Yes, it can.

"Do you have another card?"

"Do I have another card? Shit, I'm lucky to have this one. My mother had to co-sign for me to get it. But you know what? Fuck it, keep the clothes, you cracker ass . . ."

"Sorry, ma'am. Will that be all?"

"Well . . . you got layaway?"

Layaway was invented for black folks. A brother will lay away a house if you let him.

"How much for that house? Three hundred thousand? How about I give you eight dollars right now and four dollars a month. I'll be living there in no time."

Black people always brag about the shit they have on layaway. They don't even *own* it, but they're already bragging.

"That's a nice watch you got there. Wait till I get my watch outta layaway. Yeah, I got some shoes on layaway, too. I can get *one* out if I want to—but you know, *I just don't feel like it*."

You ever go window-shopping with somebody just to look at their layaway?

"There you go right there . . . yeah, five more months. Mine's is just like that only mine's is blue."

I once put a coat on layaway in September, knowing I couldn't get it out until March. When I finally got it paid off, the weather had warmed up. But I didn't care. I was determined to wear my coat for at least two months. By June, I was the only guy on the street in a parka and a pair of shorts.

THE PRICE IS RIGHT

My mother was real cheap. OK, practical. She would never pay a bill on time.

"If they ain't cuttin' it off, I ain't paying."

She would say, "The first bill is a suggestion. If they really want you to pay it, then they'll come down to your house and tap on your window."

Her whole philosophy of life was: if you die owing money, then you've won.

She wouldn't pay until the light man had his hand on the

switch. Then she'd write a check *with attitude*, like the service guy was picking on her. She'd fuss at him: "Here's your money. You act like it's *your* electricity. Were my lights bothering you? Why did you have to get involved? You need to mind your business."

My mother would make utility companies crazy because she would never pay the whole bill. Somehow she knew exactly how much money it cost just to keep things on.

Light bill's $98?

Thirty-four ought to cover it.

It was the same with the phone. I'm not sure why we had a phone. It hung alongside the big wooden spoon and fork that decorated the kitchen wall—and it was about as useful.

Sometimes the bill was so overdue that we could take calls but we couldn't make them. Then it got worse: we could take calls but we couldn't hear what anybody was saying.

"I can't hear you. Call at the corner."

I knew the corner store's number by heart.

FOR LOVE OR MONEY

My parents were both cheap. I'm sure that's why they got married in the first place. They weren't in love. They just realized, "We could save a lot of money if we was together."

To my father, everything was really made out of money. If you broke something, you broke that amount of money. If I knocked over my soda at the movies, he would say, "Hey, you just spilled a dollar. That's a damn dollar."

I'd say, "That's not a dollar, Daddy, that's a soda."

Then he'd point to the floor like he was in a Sprint commercial: "I gave you a dollar for a soda. Now look at the drops rolling down the aisle: one cent, two cent, three cent, four cent, five cent. Pick up my change, boy."

When my family went to a restaurant, it was like they had six kids but only four kids' worth of money. My parents could order whatever they wanted. The kids had to get something inexpensive. Like rice.

My father would splurge and get shrimp. I didn't have my own shrimp until I was 25 years old. If I said, "Daddy, can I have one of your shrimp?" He'd say, "No, boy. These are *poison*. They would kill a nine-year-old. I'd like to give you a piece, but it might make your head explode. Let me try one out."

Then he'd take a bite. "Yum. Alllmmmmost died."

My father grew up so poor that he would wake up at three in the morning, in a cold sweat, with "poor flashbacks." My mother would say, "Baby, what's wrong?" He would say, "I dreamed I was eating a dirt sandwich."

Now, I'm sure that everybody reading this book has been broke at some point, but few people have been hungry. My father grew up hungry. I'm not talking about when you skip breakfast and you feel a little sluggish. That's not hungry.

I'm talking about being so hungry that you can't watch TV because when the food commercial comes on you can't stop yourself from biting the screen.

I'm talking about when you haven't seen food in so long that instead of Dominos Pizza, you call UNICEF.

I'm talking about being so hungry that I might bite off your lip on a kiss.

People who've been hungry can get a little crazy and put food on a pedestal. That was my father. He didn't believe in throwing food away. He'd tell us over and over: "Food ain't garbage."

If you poured out sour milk, he'd say, "What's the matter? You never heard of yogurt?" or "Hey, boy, save that moldy bread. You never know when you might have the clap and need penicillin."

At night, before we went to bed, he'd gather us all around the garbage can while he picked through it. Better not be any food in the garbage.

"Cigarette butt, beer can, Epsom salts box, chicken—hey, wait a minute. A piece of chicken? A thigh!? I can't believe it." Then he'd call for my brother. "Andre, come here. Bring your black ass here! Did you throw away this chicken?"

"Yeah, Daddy."

"Well, I be damned! Now didn't you ask me if you could have another piece of chicken? And didn't I say, 'Yeah, you can have another piece of chicken—but are you *sure* you're gonna eat it?' And what did you say?"

"I said, 'I'm gonna eat it.' "

"Well, guess what. You're gonna eat it! So dig your hand in there and get that chicken. And don't throw away the bone! I got a sack of them in the basement. When I get enough, I'm gonna glue 'em together and make me a work bench."

My mother is the kind of woman you don't want to be in line behind at the supermarket. She has coupons for coupons. And she didn't mind driving an extra hour if she could buy something for fifty cents less than at the neighborhood market.

My mom would buy vats of stuff, too. She used to get potato sacks full of chicken wings. The wings were so tiny though, we suspected that the butcher was raiding pigeon coops.

To save pennies, my mother would rarely buy brand-name foods. We'd ask her if we could get some Jif peanut butter. She'd say, "You got some Jif money?"

We spent most of our shopping time in the no-frills aisle. You ever see the no-frills food? The white boxes, the black letters: **RICE**. No uncle, no riverboat, just rice. You look at the back of the box for the list of ingredients and it says look at the front of the box.

Same with cereal. White box, black letters: **CEREAL**. No captain on that ship, nothing lucky about those charms. . . .

One time my mother bought a can of beans. White can, black letters: **BEANS**. My brothers and I couldn't take it anymore. So we got a Magic Marker and jazzed up the can. Soon it said, **BIG-ASS BEANS**.

Next time we went to the market we said, "Mom, can we get some Big-Ass beans?"

She said, "You got some Big-Ass money?"

The cheapest my mother ever got was when she bought peanut butter with jelly *in the same jar*. How low can you go? You don't get any cheaper than that. That's like buying shoes with the socks built in. Call them *shocks*. "Put your shocks on, boy."

However, once in a while my mother would splurge and buy some brand-name foods. But it would be a brand we'd never heard of. My brothers and I would look at each other, shake our heads, and say:

"Damn. I didn't know Nipsey Russell made waffles."

"Hey, check out these Ashford & Simpson fish sticks."

"Wow. Lou Rawls got chocolate-chip cookies. Look at what the box says: 'You'll never find a bigger chip than mine.' "

There's too much food in America. We've got so much food that America's the only country in the world that makes people feel bad for being too fat.

The only country in the whole world.

Meanwhile, people are starving all over. If you're fat anywhere but in America people say, "Damn, how do you do that? That's amazing. I've got to hang with you."

We've got so much food in America, we're even allergic to it. How could someone be allergic to food? Do you think anybody in Rwanda is lactose intolerant? Only in America do you hear bullshit like, "Don't eat red meat. Red meat will kill you." What do you mean? Red meat won't kill you. Green meat will.

If you're one of the chosen few people on this planet who's lucky enough to get your hands on a steak—bite the shit out of it.

I inherited my parents' cheapness. I don't like owing anybody anything. I pay off the credit cards every month. I bought my car with cash. I *do* owe a bank for my house, but the mortgage process was very intimidating. I felt like I was dealing with the Mafia. I have thirty years to pay off the loan, and yet I still feel like somebody from the bank could come to the house at any time, tap on the window and say, "You know that money we loaned you? If you don't pay it back tomorrow, we're gonna break your fucking legs."

GET OUT!

How can a brother own two cars and *still* live with his mamma? Even if you've got one car—get out!

Guys who won't move out are a sad phenomenon. Women sometimes *have* to stay until they're old. It can be kind of cute. But men? Get out! I have 35-year-old friends who still live at home. Get out! There's only one thing worse than a man that old still living with his parents, and that's any woman willing to sneak into his room. Once you get past a certain age, you shouldn't be tiptoeing past anybody.

"Shh, take off your shoes."

Later, they're having sex and he grunts, "Say my name!"

But before she can say, "Gregory," he cuts her off: "No! Whisper it. I don't want to wake my parents."

I don't visit my friends who won't move out. Do you know how depressing it is to sit in the same room you two sat in when you were both 14? There's the little-ass dresser, the little-ass bed, and the poster of Tony Dorset on the wall.

Get out!

You can always tell when they're not planning to leave because they start doing renovations. "I'ma knock this wall out, put in a fish tank, some mirrors. Did you know mirrors make a room seem bigger?"

Some of them just try to play it off: "But I'm just taking care of moms." Bullshit. You can't take care of yourself. Your mom could make some money renting the room if you got the fuck out.

The saddest ones are the brothers waiting for their parents to die.

"Well, you know this is all gonna be mine."

What? Your mother's only 54. What are you going to do, poison her?

iT'S ALL iN THE FLASH

Whether we have money or not, black folks tend toward the flashy.

My father never made a lot of money, but he used to flash his roll whenever he had the chance. Buy a pack of gum? Pull out the roll. He could have just pulled out a dollar, but no.

White people make money to live a better life. Black people make money to pump themselves up and to make other black folks feel like shit. That's why, when some brothers get a car, they *can't wait* to drive by the bus stop.

A lot of this comes from being disrespected. A brother will get extra dressed up regardless of what he's got to do because he subconsciously thinks, "This'll get me treated white."

Not treated *right*, but white.

I'm good friends with comedian Adam Sandler. He's got money, but all he wears are sweatpants and T-shirts. Every day.

If I walked around in sweatpants and T-shirts, I'd get treated like a runaway slave.

"Saturday Night Live" people always talked about how nice I dressed. I wasn't trying to make a fashion statement; I just wanted to keep the security guards off my ass. I didn't want them to treat me like shit in the place I worked—especially because I made more money than they did. But I knew that even though they'd see me coming to work six days a week, I had to be well-dressed or they'd ask me for my I.D. And when I say I.D., I'm not talking about an NBC I.D. I'm talking about a DNA sample.

I figured that if I dressed well, then the parking attendant wouldn't make a point of telling me how much it cost to park there—like I didn't have the cash or couldn't read the sign—before I handed him the keys.

"You know it's twelve dollars?"

"My truck cost thirty thousand. I don't need to hear that shit."

RiSK AND REWARD

Black people don't play the stock market.

We play the numbers.

But how do we determine what numbers to play?

Dreams.

That's right. Dreams. When I was a kid my father had a book called *The Lucky Star Dream Book*. It listed numbers next to what kind of dreams you had. If you dreamt you were falling: number 432. If you were being chased: number 938. Every morning when I woke up my father would be standing over me, and the first thing he'd say was, "What'd you dream? You had a dream, right? Don't tell me no. I saw your eyelids twitching."

But lots of times I didn't remember my dreams so I had to make up something quick.

"I dreamt about . . . my shoes, Daddy."

Then my father would pull out his book, look under shoes, turn to me, and say, "You sure it's shoes? Are you positive it was shoes? Because shoes is 536, and sneakers are 289. I don't want you messing up my money. You know I don't like to gamble."

YA GOTTA WORK FOR A LIVING

Before I got into comedy, I used to work at McDonald's making minimum wage. When your boss pays you minimum wage, that means that she doesn't care about you. She doesn't care about your Christmas, or whether your kids have shoes. And if she has the nerve to say, "How you doing?" you're tempted to tell her, "You know how I'm doing. I'm doing bad. How else can I be doing with this money you pay me?"

When she pays you minimum wage she's saying, "I would pay you less, but it's against the law."

There are people who would like to get rid of minimum wage. But we have to have it, because if we didn't, some people would not get paid money. They would work all week for two loaves of bread and some Spam.

THE AWFUL TRUTH ABOUT TAXES

At Micky D's I earned $200 a week, and the tax man took out fifty. That was like kicking Monday and Friday in the ass. And what did I get for my tax money? All the free street light in the world. As far as I was concerned, they can give everybody a candle and let me keep my fifty.

But the reality is that we don't *pay* taxes.

The government *takes* them.

You get your check and the taxes are gone. It was not an option. The government doesn't trust you with your own money.

IRS: Gotta take it.
YOU: Why?
IRS: You might spend it.
YOU: It's mine.
IRS: No, it ain't.

I wouldn't mind paying taxes if the government did something good with the money. That would be different. Instead, they just fuck up year after year. If people fuck up with money you give them, you shouldn't have to give them more.

But every week they take money out of my check. Then they want some more money in April. What kind of gangster shit is that? Why didn't they just take the money they needed in the first place, instead of coming to me like a damn crackhead saying, "Remember that money I borrowed before? I need a little bit more; we fucked up on the budget and everything, but . . ."

It's disgraceful. Uncle Sam is on the pipe.

EVERYBODY'S GOT TO PAY

No matter how broke you are, there's a tax for you. If you work at McDonald's making fries, they tax you. I think its obvious that if you make french fries for a living that you deserve a break—**TODAY!**

But no. You still have to pay taxes. It's not fair. If you're the mop-up boy at a peep show, it's obvious the government is not working for you.

Let's get rid of taxes. Taxes are why we left England. White people said, "They're taxing everything. Let's go." That was over 300 years ago. They thought they were doing a good thing. Now taxes are even higher.

And there's no place left to go.

It's really outrageous that we have to pay taxes for services we don't even use. Like the police. I've never called a cop in my life. If some shit goes down, I have a gun. I'll handle it. And if I ever need the police I'll be glad to write them a check.

"Someone broke into my house. Here you go."

Fire department? My house isn't burning. I keep the sprinklers on 24-7-365. I keep the house nice and moist. I'm just trying to save some money.

But the government keeps taking it.

There's school tax. I don't have kids. Why am I paying school tax when I have no kids? I wore a condom for a reason: I wanted to save a few dollars. But now I have to pay for everyone else's kids to go to school? I don't give a fuck about someone else's kids. I don't care if their teacher is a basset hound. Or a duck. I don't care if your kid's in tenth grade with coloring books.

When I get some kids, I'll care. And then I'll pay.

And why do I have to pay Social Security tax?

I won't get the money until I'm 65. Meanwhile, the average black man dies at 54. It's a scam. Black people just don't live that long: hypertension, high blood pressure, L.A.P.D., something will get you. Black people should be able to get Social Security at 30. Even if I live longer, I won't need the money when I'm 65. I need the money now. Right now. I got some furniture at Macy's I need to get off layaway.

THE ONLY THING WORSE THAN TAXES

Who thought up insurance? What a scam. Why do they even call it "insurance?"

They should call it **In Case Shit Happens . . .**

The only reason I give an insurance company money is in case shit happens. When shit doesn't happen, shouldn't I get my money back? How do they manage to keep your money? I eat right. I jog. I'm not dead. *Nothing happened.* Give me my money! Don't spend it on sick people, give it back! If they'd told me they were keeping the money, I would have gone ahead and had an accident. If we knew we'd get the money back, people would stay in better shape. It would cost insurance companies less. But do they want that? Do they want you to stay in better shape?

No. They just want your money.

I don't get it. We cover the government with all our taxes, shouldn't they cover us for staying healthy?

But no. Everyone's got to have medical insurance. No one will touch you without it. One time I walked into the doctor's office with blood coming out of my head.

DOCTOR: What you got?

ME: Blood coming out of my head.

DOCTOR: No. What kind of *coverage* do you got? What insurance? We'll worry about your ailment later.

When I was a kid we didn't have insurance. My father would wait until the last minute to take us to the hospital. We had to be *real, real sick* to go to the hospital. We had to be in pain. We had to have some new disease. We had to be turning another color.

MOM: **The boy's orange.**
DAD: **Okay. Let's take him to the hospital.**

We had to be so bad off that my father would look at you and say, "Damn. The Robitussin didn't handle it."

My dad tried Robitussin for everything. We went through a lot of Robitussin when I was young. I broke my leg one time. My daddy poured Robitussin on it. Massaged it into my knee.

"Can you walk *now*?"

THE HYPOCRITICAL OATH

My dad had a point. Doctors are fucked up. They charge you all that money and they don't do shit.

Think about the last time you went to the doctor. The nurse does everything. She takes your temperature, your blood pressure. She asks you what you've got, reads your chart. Everything. At the end, the doctor comes in:

"How you feel? Here's the pills."

Doctors shouldn't get paid so much. Being a doctor is like helping out God; like being a preacher. That's how they should get paid: pass around the plate. Whatever you get, keep it and shut up.

In ancient times, doctors didn't charge money. After all, they weren't as important or as skilled at their jobs as, say, a blacksmith. They did it for free. But now, for a doctor to put a piece of wood on your tongue: "That'll be one hundred dollars."

When a doctor tells you he has to operate, he says, "And you won't be able to work for three months."

YOU: But I got to pay you back. How am I supposed to pay your ass?

Doctors charge you for delivering a kid. What happens if you don't pay? Will he shove the kid back in?

Charging people for health is low. Only a low person would charge to give a little kid a new liver. When you see a mom on TV begging, "Little Cal needs a liver so bad. Please send money. Please," notice that she doesn't say, "send a liver." No. They've already got a whole truckload of livers. They've got livers up the ass. Liver hats. Liver paperweights. Liver earrings. She says "send money" because there's a scumbag doctor out there who won't operate until he gets a check.

The only reason doctors should get paid is if they **cure** something. But they don't cure nothing. Diseases are just piling up. The same diseases have been around since I was a kid.

You think we're going to cure AIDS?

No.

They can't even cure athlete's foot.

What have they got for AIDS? A condom? The most deadly disease ever, and all they could come up with is a piece of plastic on your dick? I could have gone to a mechanic for that advice.

Hold on. Time out. **Please, you still have to wear your condom**.

A lot of guys say they do. They don't.

Nobody wears condoms all the time. Especially for that get-up-in-the-morning fuck. That "Hey, what you doing? Hey, hey . . ."/"Just turn over" fuck. Guys don't wear condoms when they should because in the time it takes to put one on a woman could change her mind.

Don't want that.

As soon as a woman hears the foil packet being ripped, and the crinkle of the plastic, she snaps back to her senses. The noise sounds like a bag of chips. But she knows there are no chips coming.

"Was I going to fuck you? Good thing I heard that plastic."

Nothing's been cured in my lifetime. Nothing. The last thing they cured was polio and that was during the first season of "I Love Lucy."

At least they're still working on AIDS. They won't cure it, but they *will* figure out a way for you to *live with it*. They won't fix it, they'll just patch it up. Their hope is that one day someone will say, "How come you weren't at work yesterday?"

"My AIDS is acting up. You know when the weather gets like this, my AIDS just pop up. But I got me some Robitussin and I'm fine now."

They don't want to cure anything because the money is in the *medicine*. It's like anything else. You think Cadillac can't make a car that lasts a lifetime? Sure they can. But there's no money in that.

"We need people to come back. We'll make a car that lasts seven years. After that, shit's gonna fall off."

Diseases are just piling up. People still got cancer, sickle cell, tuberculosis, Jerry's kids still limping around.

Cure some shit. Get rid of it.

One cool thing about AIDS is that at least they're still working it. On some diseases they've just given up.

Deafness. You go deaf, they've got nothing. No pill. Nothing. You tell a doctor you can't hear and all he can say is, "Why don't you take this little speaker and shove it in your head."

"What kind of cure is a speaker in my fucking head? Where's the science? Where's the medicine? A speaker in my head? I coulda went to the Stereo Warehouse for a speaker."

Paralysis. When you can't move, you're desperate for a cure.

YOU: Doc, I can't walk. What you got for me?

DOCTOR: Why don't you get this chair and roll around.

YOU: Where the fuck is the science, where's the medicine, where's the pill? Something? A fucking chair, a rolling chair? What kind of primitive, prehistoric shit is this? I said I can't walk, I didn't say I can't sit.

Blindness. You can't see, neither can they—a cure, that is.

YOU: Hey, Doc, I'm blind.

DOCTOR: Why don't you take this dog and have this dog drag your blind ass around.

YOU: What kind of cure is a dog? Where's the science, where's the medicine? A dog? There's people who can see that can't handle a dog. Come on man, at least give me a midget or something.

DRiVE, i SAiD

Car insurance is the worst. It's almost like the government is mad that you've got a new car. "What makes Chris think he should drive a Lexus? We're gonna get his ass."

How come you can't just buy a car and drive it off the lot? No, you've got to register it. Why do you have to register the car? To prove it's yours? Isn't your receipt good enough? Registration is just a way for the government to get paid *again*.

Did you ever find the car of your dreams and think, "I'm going to get this. This is my car. I can't wait to get in it."

Then they tell you how much insurance is.

"I'm going to get something else."

Or—you start thinking of all sorts of illegal ways to get the car. "I can register this in my grandma's name. She lives in Albuquerque, New Mexico, so I'll have an out-of-state plate. And she's got a wooden leg, so I can have a handicap plate. Every time I get out of the car I'll have to remember to drag my foot and limp, but I don't mind. I'm just gonna love my Lexus."

PRICE OF DEATH

All this complaining about the price of living.

Oh yeah? The price of death will kill you, too. There are people living now just because they cannot afford to die. They're broke, working two jobs. I know a guy who teaches and drives a cab. He's 89 years old. Every time I see him he says, "Got some good tips today. As soon as I save up enough money I'm going to drop dead."

One of my great uncles died and I had to go with my grandmother to the funeral parlor. Ever meet an old person who doesn't know anymore how much shit *really* costs because they bought everything they own 50 years ago? That's my grandmother. She hasn't bought sheets for 40 years. All she buys now are milk, eggs, and Epsom salts.

I took her to the funeral parlor. Funeral directors are the lowest people on earth. And the worst salesmen. They don't really have to *sell* you anything. They *know* you're there to buy. No one walks into the funeral parlor just to browse. There's no window-shopping. No one says, "Hey, call me when the ninety-eights come in."

The whole relationship between you and a funeral director starts off with a lie.

YOU:	You know, my great uncle died, I'm here to make arrangements.
FUNERAL DIRECTOR:	Sorry to hear that.

It's a lie. He's not sorry to hear that. He's *happy*. The only thing that could make him happier is if your great aunt had died, too. They don't want anyone to live, except their own. If a funeral director's kid saves another kid's life, the little hero is going to get a beating when he comes home.

"What the fuck is wrong with you saving somebody's life? You see somebody choking, you let 'em *choke*. You want to go to college, don't you?"

We tried to pick out a coffin. Buying a coffin is like buying a new car. There's a brochure. My grandmother looked at the models and said, "We'll take this one. I think Miles woulda liked this one."

How come when somebody dies, everybody goes, "I think he woulda liked this?"

What he'd like is *to be alive!*

Once my grandma picked the coffin, the funeral director asked, "How much money do you have, ma'am?"

GRANDMA:	Fifty dollars.

That's all she'd brought. You can't buy three vowels on "Wheel of Fortune" for fifty dollars.

DIRECTOR:	Why don't you try this, uh . . . cooler? Put in a couple beers. He'll have a great time.

Choosing a headstone is the same thing.

GRANDMA:	We'll take this one. I think Miles woulda liked this one.
DIRECTOR:	How much money do you have?

GRANDMA: Fifty dollars.

DIRECTOR: Why don't you try this Styrofoam headstone? We'll throw in a big Magic Marker and you can write whatever you want on it.

She took the marker and wrote: "He dead."

The only cool thing about funerals is that they're just like birthday parties: the family is together, there's all that food.

Only the body keeps fucking it up.

"Man, we could be having a good time right now if it wasn't for Miles."

NEITHER A BORROWER NOR A LENDER BE

Everybody wants to make some money and I don't blame them.

I want to make some money.

I did make some money.

Now I want to keep it to myself.

It's hard, because people will take your money.

You ever have somebody owe you money and have the nerve to wear new clothes around you? I mean *brand new clothes,* and they're pointing them out like, "Hey, look at what I done picked up."

"Well, did you see my money while you were there?"

If you lend someone money you have to get it back quickly, otherwise they get *used* to owing you money. It becomes a character trait: you have a fat friend, you have a bald friend, you have a friend who owes you about fifty dollars. This is the friend who has your money for so long that they start telling you about shit they're getting ready to buy.

When people owe you money and they don't repay it quickly, eventually you have to confront them. You have to hunt them down. You've got to turn into Baretta. You've got to walk right up into their face and say, "Didn't I give you that fifty dollars? Wasn't that you? Wasn't that me? Wasn't that my hand? Wasn't that your hand? Yes, I gave you fifty dollars."

After you go through all that, they'll say, "Man, I forgot."

Now you know that's a lie. You *know*. How the fuck can you forget where you got some free money from? You don't forget that. If you find $50 on the ground, you're going to remember that for the rest of your life. Every time you walk by that spot, you think, "That's where I found fifty dollars. Right here. April fourteenth, nineteen seventy-two. I remember, I remember. It was a cloudy day, about sixty-eight degrees, and I was wearing my black hat. I loved that hat. And it was about forty-two percent humidity outside and my momma was pregnant with Warren. And I told her, 'Don't drink when you're pregnant.' Now Warren got three toes. Anyway, this is the spot. I looked at the ground and saw ten dimes, four quarters, and a forty-eight-dollar bill."

You know what's worse than lending money?

Lending money to a woman you're fucking.

Every woman I've ever dated has owed me money. In fact, I've never met a woman who didn't need an extra thousand dollars. Some women act like you're not sharing if you don't give it to them. They act like you didn't work hard for your money. They act like it was Lotto money, and if you got lucky, so should they—just like they think you got lucky when they let you fuck them.

So don't do it. Especially if the woman you're going out with is fine. It's going to cost you. A fine woman has to get her hair done, her body waxed, her nails manicured, and a facial. Twenty-five percent of her fineness comes from money.

Plus, fine women just spend more, anyway. She spends and spends and figures everything is going to work out—because she's fine. A fine woman knows that nobody in their right mind is going to throw her out on the street.

So just don't lend money to someone you're fucking.

But I know you will. It's probably already too late, right?

Okay, then just don't try to get your money *back*. Why? Because your woman thinks the sex she's giving you is the payback. I dare anyone reading this to *try* to get back the money. Go on. Just step up to her and say, "Hey, babe. What's up with that two hundred you owe me?"

Then step back quickly because she'll give you a *look* and say, " 'Scuse me? I think I paid you last night. Matter of fact, you owe *me* one-fifty."

LOVE, SEX, BROCCOLI AND CHEESE

New love is like discovering a new favorite food. At first, it's all you want. It's all you need. When I was a kid, I fell in love with broccoli and cheese. It was my favorite flavor in the world. Didn't understand why. Didn't matter. My mother understood and she made it for me all the time. Green Giant Broccoli & Cheese; the kind that came in the plastic pouch. You just put it in a pot of boiling water. I had to have that broccoli and cheese.

Then one day I didn't want any more broccoli and cheese. I put it in my mouth and my mouth rejected it like a stolen credit card. I never imagined that would happen. I thought I *loved* broccoli and cheese. But no. Now I nearly throw up at the sight of broccoli and cheese. In fact, to me, the words "broccoli and cheese" are a curse. You can walk up to me and say "Shut up, motherfucker," and I won't do anything. But if you say "broccoli and cheese" I'll punch you in the face.

Still, I learned a lesson from broccoli and cheese that I'll never forget: no matter how in love you are, no matter how much you think something's going to last forever, no matter how fine the woman is, there's a guy out there who's tired of fucking her. And if you're with her now, chances are one day *you'll* be that guy.

When you've got a love jones, you're like Mr. Magoo: legally blind, always bumping into something, and so deep up in it that you have no time for the rest of life. The landlord put your shit out in the street? So what? You're in love. Six people in the next room have the Ebola virus? You don't care. You're in love. World War III just broke out? Let 'em fight. You're in love.

The reason we say "fell in love" is that it makes it sound more like an accident. Men act like, "I was walking along and fell in love. I tried to get my boys to pull me out, but I got all tangled in ropes and sticks and I couldn't break free."

Love can be cool if a woman falls in there with you. But that doesn't always happen. More often than not you'll fall in by yourself. You can't make somebody love you.

Want to.

Can't.

I once had a thing for this fine actress. The only reason she went out with me was because I asked her on dates she couldn't refuse.

ME: Prince and Michael Jackson are on stage together for the first time, and I think Richard Pryor is the opening act.
HER: Well, in that case . . .

But just because a woman goes out with you doesn't mean she likes you. Sometimes she just wants to get out of the house.

If a woman *really* wants to be with you she won't care where you take her.

> **YOU:** Would you like to go to the Spam convention?
> **HER:** Sure!

But what did I know? I sent her flowers. I took her to "Saturday Night Live." I also gave her money and helped her make some connections. I even let her move into my house and told her she didn't have to sleep with me.

Okay, that last part's not true, but I did like her enough to help her get a movie role. To her, I was like Babyface to the third power. I got off on the fact that she was a real actress and not just somebody in a Teddy Riley video who was prepared to fuck John Singleton for a part in *Poetic Justice II*. I even went to see her in one of those downtown productions—a play with a bunch of naked people, chanting. Can you picture me in the audience? Yes, I pulled out *all* the stops. But if she got my message she didn't exactly act like she'd read it.

Finally, I had to tell her the truth:

"Hey, I'm in love with you."

As soon as I said the words I realized that she couldn't give a fuck. I knew because her voice got all sweet and patient.

"It's not you," she told me. "It's just that right now I'm not ready for a relationship."

I knew *that* line. That's what all women tell you when you're not *the guy*. What it really means is, "You know what? I just can't imagine fucking you. I have fantasies of fucking men all the time, but none of them ever involve you. I'm sure there will be a woman out there who loves your scrawny ass, but I'm not her."

If you hear a woman say, "It's not you," guess what?

It's *always* you!

If I was the guy, there'd be no excuse for her not to be in the relationship. When it comes to love, women don't give a shit about the odds against it. Pocahontas fell in love with John Smith while his boys were slaughtering her family. Romeo and Juliet's people were feuding for generations, and they still tried to make a go of it. Women *love* to be in relationships.

When a woman meets *the guy* she's ready.

TAKE A HiNT

Being blown off is bad. Not getting the hint is worse.

When a woman puts you off, you have to move on. Go cold turkey. I know, you still want to reach out and touch. You just can't help it. But the surest way to debase yourself—and one of the saddest things—is to keep calling all the time, trying to create a coincidence.

> HER: Hi.
> YOU: Happy Arbor Day! I was just thinking about you.
>
> HER: Hello.
> YOU: It's Sherman Hemsley's birthday. I thought I'd call.
>
> HER: Yes?
> YOU: I was looking up at the sky, and noticed it was blue. I remembered you had a blue shirt—so I figured I'd check in.
>
> HER: What now?
> YOU: I was just drinking water and I remembered there was water at your house.

Believe me, she really doesn't want to talk to you.

THE FRIEND ZONE

If you have a job and a life and you date a woman with a job and a life, after a couple of months you should be having sex. You're both busy people, so it *can* take time.

If you're working and she's not, then you should be having sex after about a month.

If neither of you works, you should have sex after about three hours. Maybe sooner. What else do you have to do?

In any case, you *must* establish that you have a dick, early on. By the second date you should make an attempt to fuck her. Your intent is not really to score, just to make her realize, "If we're gonna hang out, eventually I'm going to have to fuck this guy." In football terms, it means you have to have a running game or the pass will never work. And if you get lucky and reach the end zone quickly, you can do a little dance afterward in the shower, and spike the shampoo bottle.

But no matter how many jobs you've got, if nothing's happened in two months, she just doesn't think of you sexually. Even worse, you've hung around too long.

It's not always easy to be sure. If you make your move early and she says, "We shouldn't," or "We can't," or even the stern, "No!" it *still* may happen someday. You owe it to yourself and all men to try again.

But if you hear, "Come on, we're pals. Let's not mess this up," or, "I don't want to ruin our friendship," then all you've got is friendship—and you've wasted two months that you could have spent with a woman who *wanted* to have sex with you.

I once dated a woman for three months, and we barely kissed. For some reason I just thought things were happening kind of slowly. That was okay. I really liked her, and now and then you have to be the sensitive guy.

Then, one night after a date, we stood in front of her building. I looked up at her apartment window. I gazed into her eyes. My eyes said, "Wonder when I'm gonna get *in* there?"

I didn't even have to open my mouth for her to know it was time to break it down.

> HER: You like me. I like you. It's cool.
> ME: Right.
> HER: We have a good time.
> ME: Yeah.
> HER: But I just I don't like you like *that*. (quickly) So let's be real. It's been three months. I figure you must be fucking around. I know I am . . .

"*I know I am?*" Wow. It was so weird for a girl to be *that* straight with me that all I could think was, "She's the coolest, ever." I stayed low-key and said goodbye, but in my head I was so turned on by her honesty that I think I love her to this day.

If you hang around a woman long enough and don't seem to mind that you're not getting naked, you can become a platonic friend. Men don't have platonic friends—as a choice. We have women we haven't fucked.

Yet.

Men think, "As soon as I figure this out, I'm in there."

Women say, "He's my pal, he's my bud, he's my *platonic* friend. I love him like a brother."

If men have platonic friends, it's by accident. Men are just not built that way. We do whatever it takes to perpetuate the race. Being platonic friends only perpetuates long walks and longer talks.

I know a couple women who are my platonic friends. But it didn't start out that way. I tried to fuck them, made a wrong turn, and ended up in the Friend Zone. There, no matter how much she likes you, you're a dickless man. It's where you end up doing dumb things like taking her to the movies, taking her to dinner, to miniature golf, and the drugstore to get condoms . . . before dropping her off at some other guy's house.

You guys know who you are.

Women can get rid of a girlfriend every six months, but they keep platonic friends forever.

Why? *Because you never know.*

YOU: What happened to Cherie?
HER: She thought she was so cute.

But she holds on to the platonic friends.
Why? *Because you never know.*

YOU: What happened to Carol?
HER: Can't hang with that bitch.

But she'll always hang with her platonic friends.
That's right: *Because you never know.*

Women can have platonic friends because they alone understand the mystical concept. Men don't know how it works . . . exactly.

Here, for the first time in print, is the mysterious bottom line: to a woman, a platonic friend is like a **dick in a glass case**.

In Case Of Emergency Break Open Glass!

Fellas, every woman has a platonic friend, and if you mess up, that's whose shoulder she'll cry on.

Sniffling, hugging him, she says, "I can't believe this happened. I'm so glad you're here."

Next thing you know, they're hitting it. That's right, hitting it! Hitting it hard! "Oh, that feels so good . . ."

Here's the sad part: You already know the next man who's

gonna fuck your woman. You've met him. He's been at your house, he's eaten your food, drunk your wine . . . and he shall betray you.

BE ALL THAT YOU CAN'T BE

A big key to getting a woman is to know what you look like.

The problem is that most guys never do. We think we can treat women like our best-looking friend treats them. But we can't get away with the same shit. Why? Because *he's* good-looking.

I've got a friend named Al who can walk around all day in a T-shirt and jeans. He has muscles. He looks great. My skinny ass has to put on a suit.

I've got a friend named Mike. He shaved his head. But Mike can do that. His head is round. My bald head looks like a yam with chicken pox.

Fortunately, many women also don't know how *they* really look. For the ladies reading this, good news! You can give yourself a test. Just a little test, don't be scared. Here it is: if you've been over to a guy's house more than four times, been fucked every time, and haven't met anybody in the house—he doesn't think you look that good. If every time you go over all you see is one room, it's a sign.

HER: But I got to pee.
HIM: Hold it in.

You've got to know what you look like. The sad part is that when you finally do, you realize you can't get anybody, looking like you do.

You have to look better than you look. You have to dress better than you dress. You have to act better than you act. You have to be smarter than you really are. You have to sing better, be more sensitive. You've got to inflate everything about yourself. Then you've got to keep up the act. But it's hard to keep up the act because it's a lie.

The whole mating dance is a big lie. And, from head to toe, women are masters of the lie. Her hair isn't really like that. She's not really that tall. She doesn't really smell that way. She's got paint all over her face. You can get her home and get her clothes off and fall into bed, but when you finally look up, you're with a whole other person. Meanwhile, the woman you brought in is tossed on a chair and scattered all over the floor.

Men tell lies, too. We're great liars. Then one day when we think it's safe—or we can't take it anymore—we blurt out the truth:

"Hey, remember that guy you fell in love with? He's dead. But I'm here if you need me."

SHE'S UGLY BUT SHE SURE CAN COOK

A woman can fall in love with an ugly man and admit it. She can show him off to all her friends and the family—even if he's the ugliest guy in the world. She'll be proud of the ugly man, hold his hand, drag him all around, introduce him to people. "This is Kevin. I want you to meet Kevin. I know he's not that attractive. But he's *good to me*."

Women are cool like that. Guys aren't. A man will never admit to being in love with an ugly woman. He will hide that to the death. He's telling nobody.

Men have women we'll fuck—but we won't take them out.

"You want to go out? Well, you're out. You're out of your bed and into my bed at my house."

Guys are full of shit. That's mean, right? We have women we'll fuck but we *won't take out*!

Women are just as mean.

You've got men you let take you out . . . but you won't fuck. There are guys on dates right now who aren't getting any, and never will. Someone's spending big dough in some restaurant and on some show, but it's still no go. Not going to work.

That's the problem with men: we always think we can *buy* sex. "If I take her here she'll give me some. If I buy her this she'll give me some."

Nothing gets you nothing.

A woman knows if she's going to fuck you within the first five minutes of meeting you. Women know right away. Women know on the handshake. As they grip your hand, if they like you, they're thinking, "I'm going to fuck him. I hope he doesn't say anything stupid."

Listen up, men: women are all about the mood. If a woman's in the mood and she wants you, just shut up and let it happen. If you say something wrong those panties will come up mighty fast.

> HIM: What team did Malcolm X play for?
> HER: What'd you say? Excuse me?

Then she has to phone her girlfriend the next day.

"Yeah, I was going to give him some, but he started talking. Just talking, yakkety, yak. I hate a yakking man."

IT'S THE SWERVE

Let's say that despite all the obstacles, you've found the woman for you—the woman of your dreams. Now you have to ask yourself the big question: are you for her?

Women are very clear when it comes to the kind of men they like. They go for guys with a little edge, a little swerve. They want somebody who's cool and street, but sophisticated and fine. No wonder men have it worse than women. She can be average and still connect. Any woman can get a guy if she really wants one.

But he has to have it *all* going on.

Women want everything.

Guess what? They can't have everything.

Women always complain that there are no men out there. But there are plenty of guys. The problem is that women all go after *the same men*. Ninety percent of the women fuck ten percent of the men. Let me put that more clearly: **You all want to fuck the same guys.** Meanwhile, most men aren't getting shit. Most men are just waiting around, wondering, "When am *I* going to get laid?"

All women want the go-getter. The conqueror. But after he's made the conquest they get mad because he won't stick around.

What did you expect? He's got to conquer more. He knows he's got a great responsibility to all women. They depend on him. He's their fantasy.

But a woman doesn't want to hear that. As soon as Mr. Wonderful moves on, she's on the phone with her girlfriend wanting to know why all men are *so full of shit*.

It's not all men, just that ten percent who are lucky enough to fuck the ninety percent.

A good rule of thumb: if a guy's got two cars, he's fucking two women. If he's got three, he's fucking everybody.

Women want men with "swerve." A man's version of "swerve" is a woman who's "fine." That's what we want. That's always Plan A. But men are practical. If we can't get the fine ones, we'll move quickly to Plan B. Can't be with a woman who's a ten? You go for two fives. Or five twos. Adds up to the same thing. Personally, I draw the line at ten ones. We're talking self-respect here.

Sometimes you get it, but it's too late. I once had a crush on this girl who lived on my block. We had a lot in common. She liked me, but I was never really cool enough for her. I tried to get with her for four years, without much success. Then I went on "The Joan Rivers Show." It was my first TV break. Right away she slept with me. Wow. Made me happy and miserable at the same time. If she had slept with me a month before the show, that would have been fine. But she slept with me after. It was like, *damn.*

Everybody wants a person who's into *them.* I always wanted someone to want me for being Chris—not for being the famous guy on TV. But I'll never know who's really down with me unless I'm so broke I'm trying to mail letters with food stamps.

But I'm doing Okay. Everybody's your friend when you're doing Okay.

You know who knows who his real friends are?

Vanilla Ice.

WHiTE GiRLS

Yes, things are going great. I do comedy specials. Movies. Albums. Got a new TV show.

You know what's next?

Right. White girls.

Got to get a white girl. You're not a successful black man without a white girl. They won't even let you buy a mansion without a white girl.

| BLACK MAN: | Here's your million dollars. |
| REAL ESTATE AGENT: | Where's your white girl? We have zoning restrictions. |

You know what's funny? If you're black and you go out with a white girl, everything that goes wrong in your life gets blamed on the white girl.

"Hey man, I hear Chris got hit by a bus."

"Going out with a white girl."

"Yeah, I hear Chris broke his leg."

"White girl. That's what he gets."

Even if you don't have the swerve, when you date a white woman, just being black is enough. To a white woman, every brother has edge and swerve. You could be as goofy as Urkel, but to a white woman, you're a wild man.

People should date who they like. I believe in chemistry. If it works, go for it. But there are white girls who only go out with black guys. And there are black girls who only go out with white guys. The first way is okay with me, of course, but if I see a fine sister with a white guy, I get pissed. I don't get violent, but I get mad. I see a fine sister with a white guy and I'm thinking, "Hey baby, what do I got to do to get with you? What must I do?"

Remember the black ice skater, Debbie Thomas? She married a white guy. Walked down the aisle and married him. I was mad at first. I thought, "Damn, Debbie. What do I got to do to get with you?" But then I thought it over and realized that she probably didn't meet many brothers on the ice.

No brothers skating by saying, "Hey, what's up, girl. Yeah, I got tickets to the Snoop Doggy Dogg show."

I once asked out a fine sister. She turned me down.

> HER: Sorry. I don't date black men.
> ME: Girl, how come you don't date black men?
> HER: No reason.
> ME: No reason?

So I punched her in the face. Now she's got a reason.

Okay, I didn't really do that. I'm not really violent or intolerant. Especially if I see a white guy with an ugly sister. My first thought is, "Hey, thanks a lot, man. Thanks for taking her ugly ass off our hands, because we didn't know what we were going to do about her."

GRADING ON A CURVE

A man should never ask a woman how many men she's slept with.

Why?

Because you don't want to know.

Just be happy you're fucking her now. It's not too much to ask. It's better that way.

But you still want to know. Why, why, why? First of all, no

matter what number she says, it's too many. She could say two, and you'd go, "TWO? TWO! Whoo! I guess that's just how you were raised."

Women know this, so women have learned to lie about it.

Because you really don't want to know.

They'll even lie in court. They don't care. I figure you gotta give every woman a seven-dick curve. If she says, "Three," it's ten. It could be three dicks to the eighth power—which is 6,561 (go on, work it out)—but she'll still say, "Three."

And it's not because she failed arithmetic.

Women are tricky. You ask a woman how many men she's fucked, and she'll tell you how many *boyfriends* she's had instead. A woman doesn't count all the miscellaneous dick: the guy she met at the club; that time she fucked Keith Sweat; the local she dubbed in Jamaica. She figures, "That's a different country, it doesn't count. I thought we were just talking domestic dick." And she really believes it.

THAT NASTY TABOO ELEMENT

Guys, when it comes to sex, romance is more important to women. Lust is more important to us. We lust, and want to be lusted after. Women feel romantic and want romance in return. What confuses me is why women dress to inspire lust and then give us shit for forgetting the romance. What do they want to hear?

YOU: That's a . . . romantic little **dress, baby.**

HER: Thank you. How sweet.

YOU: Yeah. Now take it off. Slowly.

Guys can handle romance. We like romance. But we don't want all romance all the time. We want heat. We don't want that part to be homogenized. We need that nasty taboo element. Sure, we all want that deep feeling for somebody, but no man wants it to seem like he's fucking his mother. Or your mother. That would be *too* nasty.

But it would be interesting because your mama sure is fine!

When you're having sex, one way to make it really hot is to feel like you're doing the wrong thing.

"This is wrong? Great!"

That's why talking dirty is cool, as long as you say the right "wrong thing." Don't make comments about her teeth and gums. Also, words like "penis" and "vagina" should never come up. I once knew a woman who used to say "vagina" and think she was talking dirty because she said it LOUD! I used to call her Loud Dirty Girl.

> HER: I feel your PENIS! In my VAGINA!
> ME: Stop it. Stop it! I can't even touch you anymore.

Sometimes you're both talking dirty and *you* go too far. You say something that gets you kicked out of bed. Your woman's going: "Fuck me, fuck me, fuck me, harder, harder, fuck me . . . put your finger in my ass, fuck me . . ."

> YOU: All right, you little slut.
> HER: Who you calling a slut?

Then you've got to talk your way back into bed.

> YOU: I didn't mean slut in a bad way, I meant it as a compliment.

I'm not an expert, but if you're going to talk dirty with your woman, you've got to talk with authority. You can get a woman to do any nasty little thing you want, if you say it like a man. First, you put a little bass in your voice. You make a little eye contact. And she will do what you want.

She *wants* to do what you want.

She's **dying** to do what you want.

More importantly she *does* do what you want—only she may not be doing it with you.

That's right. Your woman is nastier than you ever imagined. But you've got to say your shit right, because if you mumble it, it's not getting done.

Don't do this:

YOU: Excuse me . . . I have a request . . . Could you lick my balls?
HER: Huh? I ain't licking nothing. Lick your own balls.

Suddenly it's a dry ball kinda day. You probably think there's nothing worse than dry balls.

Yes, there is.

Do you realize that in 1997 some women still don't give head? Ninety-fucking-seven. When I was single and I met a woman who didn't give head, I'd look at her like she was a Betamax.

"They still make you?"

When it comes to head, there's three types of women.

Woman A doesn't do it.

"Get the fuck outta here!"

Woman B gives you just enough to shut you up.

"Uh . . . well, okay." Then she takes a little lick.

Woman C is my favorite.

"Where's that dick? It's got the antidote and I'm gonna get it."

You think with all their complaining about head, that all men would eat pussy just to encourage a little reciprocation.

Some men still don't.

That's crazy. That's counterproductive. I once sucked a

woman's pussy so hard I got a hangover. If you don't eat pussy your woman's going to be gone. She'll find someone else who will.

Maybe she already has.

THE REAL MEANiNG OF NiCE

Nothing stimulates the nasty-taboo sector of a man's brain more than the sight of a beautiful woman. It opens doors. I remember one time I went to a concert with a girlfriend who was really fine. When we got there, I realized I didn't have the tickets.

I said, "Come on, let's go home."

She said, "No. Let's go *talk* to the guy at the door." So she started talking to the security guard, and pretty soon we were inside.

As we took our seats, she said, "He was nice."

Nice? We didn't get in because the guy was *nice*. We got in because she had a **nice *ass*.** A club can be packed, with another hundred people outside straining against the velvet ropes. Big, ugly doorman barks at them to get back. Then the fine girl shows up, and suddenly there's room in the club for just one more. If the woman had weighed 300 pounds, or if I had talked to the guy, it would have been a Blockbuster night for sure.

Some women are born fine and stay that way forever. Too bad. There's no one more naive than the woman who's been beautiful all her life. She naturally figures everything is going to work out. The fine girl has more options. She has a sense of entitlement.

The fine girl hears, "Yes. You can go to the party."

The fat girl hears, "Have another cookie."

If the average girl sees a commercial about Jamaica, she thinks, "Oh, that would be nice."

The fine girl thinks, "I'm going there next week."

It's best when a woman grows into her beauty. If she was a little less sure of herself coming up or didn't get her braces out until she was eighteen, she has a lot more compassion for people. She knows *exactly* how mean people can be.

But a fine-looking woman is forced by the way men treat her to understand—and quickly use—her power. And when she does, a woman can take her beauty to the bank. To a fine girl there's no such thing as the mean doorman. You know how much it would cost Naomi Campbell to go around the world?

About $40.

No. $32.50.

Women have it good, good, good.

Not that I'm complaining. Women have a lot more to think about sexually than men. Men have only one job: knock it out. That's it. Be good in bed. That's our only responsibility. Women can also be good, but sometimes they have to try not to be *too* good. Women want a man to think he's got a good woman, but they don't want him to think he's got a freak.

Their solution: ration the pussy.

This is how women think:

"Okay, I'm gonna fuck him now, but then I'm not gonna suck his dick for two weeks."

"All right I'll suck his dick now, but I won't lick his balls for the next two months."

"I'll lick his balls now, but I'm not gonna lick his ass till next year."

Men have to do all our tricks up front because we don't know if there's gonna be a return engagement.

WHAT YOU DON'T KNOW CAN STiLL HURT YOU

A woman is much more comfortable taking her current man around guys she's slept with than a guy is taking his woman around women he's had sex with. ("Slept with"/"sex with." Isn't that it in a nutshell?) Men need to believe we're the first ones in. We look at women like countries. We want to plant our flag on virgin soil. We don't want to be immigrants. It's too hard to get a green card so we can stay, and even then, collecting health and retirement benefits is questionable.

A woman can walk into a party with her man, and there'll be four guys there that she fucked—and it *will not faze her one bit*. She will introduce her man to every one of those guys, like there is nothing to it.

"I want you to meet Brad, and this is Kevin, and this is Mark, and this is Michael. They're all my friends."

But if a man is walking down the street with his woman and he sees someone he fucked in 1972, *he will cross the street*.

Women don't mind that you fucked around before you got with them, as long as from the moment you laid eyes on them your past is completely cut off. Erased from memory. And don't even think about staying friends with old girlfriends because in their own way, women *also* want to be the only one. (What? You're surprised?)

Even so, women are more generous than men when it comes to tolerating the past. Women will still let you have *some* other women in your life. She has a list: your mama, your sisters, and one ugly friend.

If I meet an old girlfriend, I already know she's thinking: "I'm not fucking you. I'm not even *thinking* about fucking you. Actually it's hard to believe I **used** to fuck you." I can see it in their faces.

Look, it's not even that a guy *wants* to fuck his old girl-friends. But he wonders: *"Can* I still fuck her? How much effort would it take? I wouldn't even try, but I'd like to know."

Men have it hard. Everywhere the average woman goes there's always some guy hitting on her, letting her know she looks good. No one tells the average man he looks good.

The only way to feel that is to fuck somebody.

That's why men cheat. All we want is to feel pretty.

I'm famous; my old girlfriends are not. But I know that the shoe could easily have been on the other foot. One night I dreamed I used to date Whitney Houston before she became a celebrity, and that I ran into her years later. She was a big star and I was working at the International House of Pancakes. There I was, busing a table, when she walked in the door.

ME: (to myself, going crazy) Shit. It's Whit. What am I going to do? Okay, I'm going to take her order, look down, and hope she won't recognize me. Hi, may I take your order?

HER: My God, Chris! What are you doing here!?!

ME: Mm-mm-m . . . my father owns the place and he's sick and . . . want some pancakes?

HER: Maybe. Oh, I want you to meet Bobby.

ME: Bobby. Hi. I love your music. You want some eggs? You want some coffee? Eh, eh, eh, eh, eh, what you up to Whitney?

HER: Got a new movie, me and Denzel . . . how about you?

ME: Well, we got some new grease here. It's real good. It only gets this good about two times a year. It really makes the pancakes sit right up. The grease is good. And we only got the milk four days ago, so . . . what you been up to? It's so good to see you again. Maybe we can go hang out sometime.

HER: Say, how about those pancakes?

ME: Did you want some coffee with that?

Most guys couldn't care less about all their old girlfriends—that is, everyone except the "relationship buster." You know who I'm talking about. Every man's got one. You dated for a minute, but you're connected for life. You grew up the same, see eye-to-eye on everything. You even *hate* the same stuff.

But you never got together.

When she broke up with a guy, she'd want to hang around with you, and that would break up your relationship. When you broke up with someone, you'd call her, and it would mess up her relationship. Why? Because you'd rather be with her.

But you never got together.

Why the hell not? Because you figured she'd *always* be there.

> HER: (with you, in bed): That was wonderful. How come . . . why do you think we never got together?
> YOU: Uh . . . I'm going to go fuck around now, okay?

But time passes, things change.
Two months later . . .

> YOU: Huh? What? You're getting married?

Now, no matter how happy you are in life, you know you'll never be totally happy. You'll always be missing something.

It's your own damn fault.

HOW TO GET A RICH MAN

A woman can fuck a man at the drop of a hat, but she can't *just* fuck him. Especially a successful man. She figures there's got to be other girls fucking him. She wants to stand out. So she has to change his life.

But how?

Domestic skills. I'm not lying.

Lots of men say they don't care if a woman lacks domestic skills.

"As long as she's fine and the sex is good, I don't mind."

So how come, if she cleans up his shit, he always notices? Before I got married, I had the Dirty Socks Rule. If a date could walk past one of my dirty socks and not pick it up or tell me something was wrong, she was out. I'm already messy. That's a given. But there's nothing more pitiful than two adults living in a dirty house. If I married a woman as messy as I am, we'd have a filthy house, a bunch of dirty kids, and a cockroach cabaret playing nightly in the kitchen. The kids would get married and we'd have dirty grandkids. A whole black family down the tubes, all because of an overlooked sock.

THE RULES OF DEPENDENCY

You know what they say about a man's stomach being the way to his heart? It's true. Sort of. Men like women who can cook because it gives them the impression she's not out there screwing a lot of guys—otherwise she wouldn't have time to cook. If she's clever, she *could* be out there every night—as long as she cooks occasionally and keeps her kitchen stocked. The sight of a kitchen with some ingredients in it gives any man that homey, secure feeling, and he's never the wiser.

Even if a woman can't cook, she should make sure her man's eating right. Make sure he's got his vegetables. That way, if he ever thinks about breaking up, he'll immediately have second thoughts. When you break up with a woman who can actually cook, in less than a week you'll feel the pain—in your stomach. The idea of not eating right, *and* filthy socks lying all over the place, is enough to conjure the fear of God.

"Shit, I don't know if I can make it on my own."

Young girls are trouble. But there's a lot to be said for older women. Not Louise Jefferson old, just older than you. Young girls are full of shit. They like what they like. They say "I want him to be this tall, want his hair to be like this, want his eyes to be like this, want him to walk like this, talk like this. . . ."

All of it's bullshit that's got nothing to do with anything.

But you find an older, single woman, and she says, "Hey, I just want a man! Got a dick and a job and I'll be happy."

You know what else? Older women cook. Young girls can only make reservations. Older women know the power of the pot on the stove. There's lots of advice out there about how to get a man, but it's really simple. Put a pot on a stove. Every day at 6:00 p.m. A man will show up. Maybe more than one, from miles around.

Let me be plain: I would take a sweet potato pie over a big ass any day. Anybody can suck a dick, but making gravy is an art.

The thing that tells a woman she's really in tight with a man is when he lets her answer his phone. All women know this. When the phone is off-limits, she figures there must be other women in the picture. At best, maybe he's not seeing other women, but he still hasn't made up his mind to close the deal with *her*. Once he lets her answer the phone, it announces to any woman who calls: "You've got his number, but I'm here—and could be here at any time. Bitch."

A man's phone is his key to the outside world. Once he lets a woman answer it, he's handed her a duplicate key.

Women, here's some important advice to remember when you get a new man: buy a new tube of KY Jelly. When a guy is poking through your medicine cabinet, nothing is going to make him think the wrong thing more than an old tube of KY Jelly rolled up like toothpaste.

"Oh, she fucks *all the time*."

Actually, he doesn't even want to see the tube. A receipt lying around will do. What men really want is to know that after you slept with him the first time you bought a tube because you're planning to do it some more.

Fellas? Seems great now. *Broccoli and cheese* later.

CHANCES ARE

This is the most important thing to know before getting involved: Relationships are very simple. Only two things can happen. You get married or you break up. That's it. There's no third thing.

Chances are you're going to break up.

That's right. Chances are you're going to break up with the person you're with right now. (The one sitting next to you, flipping channels, eating a ham sandwich while you read this.) So get a good look. This might be it. Why? Because at some point that person's going to say something just a little too ignorant for you.

> HER: What team did Malcolm X play for?
> YOU: What the fuck?

Or they'll do something you just can't overlook. For some people it's stepping over a dirty sock or suddenly admitting over breakfast that they were accused of killing their former spouse but Johnnie Cochran got them a "not guilty" verdict. Whenever the person does that thing, it registers right away as something you cannot live with for the rest of your life.

No matter what it is, it's okay to break up about it. Nothing is too petty to consider when the next thing you might have to think about is getting married.

When a relationship's over, a man will do a double-take, shake his head, pack up, and sneak out before daylight. He'll run out into the snow wearing no slippers. He just wants out.

Not a woman. Women don't tell you it's over. First they end it in their heads. Only later do they end it in words. There are three phases.

First she has to check it out with her girlfriends, especially the one girlfriend who can't stand you because she sees through all your shit and knows every lie you tell even before your woman knows it.

Next she has to test it out, survey it, think it over. "What will the repercussions be if we break up? Will my rent still get paid? What about my tuition? Can I still eat out?"

Finally, she has to find a new man. She has to locate a new dick, make sure it works.

Then she'll go to you with some sad story.

"You know, I've been trying to communicate with you for

a while and it's not working. I really think that we need to get . . . I think we should see new people."

Meanwhile, her new man's outside, in the car, blowing the horn, yelling.

"Come on. Come on! **The movie starts at nine!**"

6

i SAiD, "SHUT UP!"

Did you ever have a job you just weren't qualified for?

Suppose you found yourself in an operating room, all dressed up like a surgeon.

"Contusion? Subdural hematoma? Yeah, sure, I can handle it. Whoops . . . shouldn't have cut that. No, no, nurse. I know you're not supposed to put a Band-Aid on a heart."

Marriage is like that.

You have no fucking clue what's going on, but you kind of fake your way through it. If you're lucky, you won't get caught.

But some people still think marriage is easy. Bullshit. Marriage is the roughest thing in the world. Nelson Mandela endured 27 years in a South African prison, but once he got out, it only took two years before his marriage busted his ass. He had to decide whether to get divorced or beg to be let back into jail, just so he could have some fucking peace of mind. If Nelson Mandela can't make it, what chance do the rest of us have?

People always ask me, "Hey, Chris? How's your marriage?"

It's all right. But marriage is rough. It shouldn't be for life. Marriage should be like our driving privilege. You need a license. You have to take a test. Then five years and renew. And you have to take every test again. The written test, the blow job test . . .

Oh? Did I go too far?

Five years and renew. Please!

THE OLD GUY

When it comes to spending a life together, a woman makes up her mind quicker than a man. She goes on four good dates, and she's already thinking, "Why are we bullshitting? What are you waiting for?" A man will bullshit and wait as long as he can. He will put off the big day until he has no other choice.

Eventually he's gotta give in. There are many, many reasons.

Some men just don't want be the Old Guy in the Club. You know who I'm talking about. Go into any club and there's always one old guy, standing around, checking out the action, blinking in the strobe light, looking like he's wishing for a slow Al Green tune instead of a dance mix. He's trying to look cool but he's a bit uncomfortable. He's not *really* old, just a little *too old* to be alone in a club.

Other guys give in not because they're ready to get married, but because they just don't want to break up.

"Shit. Who's gonna make my dinner and pick up my dirty socks?"

So he doesn't settle down, he surrenders.

"All right, all right, I'll marry your ass. Damn. OK, just tell me the day before and I'll be there." Then he shrugs his shoulders and says to himself, "I guess this is it."

Maybe that's why there's so much divorce today: Because of all the times someone has said, "Okay, I guess this is it."

JUST LiKE MEAT?

Women and relationships: easy to get into, hard to maintain, hard to get out of. If you knew you'd have a rough time ending things, then why'd you move in together in the first place? Starting a relationship is like buying a cellular phone: they let you in real easy. You can get one real cheap. But one day that bill will bust your ass.

For a while, a relationship can be great. You don't have to think anymore about going out alone at night. You don't have to feel insecure. You eat right and the place is clean. You're finally past the same old games—and into new ones. Oh, well.

One problem is that the longer you're in a relationship, the more you've compromised yourself. It starts off with something as simple as eating in a vegetarian restaurant—when you're not vegetarian. You're already in a funk by the time you arrive because you've just been through that whole "looking for a place to eat" thing.

YOU: Where should we eat?
HER: I don't know. What do you think?
YOU: It doesn't matter. Anything you like.

HER: I can't decide. You pick.
YOU: Whatever you want.
HER: It's up to you.

Finally, you get out the door.

RESTAURANT NO. 1: "I can't eat here."
RESTAURANT NO. 2: "I don't think so."
RESTAURANT NO. 3: "This won't work, either."

At each place you see perfectly healthy people enjoying themselves. Meanwhile you're driving an extra 20 miles so your woman can get a fucking rice cake. You try your best to suck in your anger.

HER: Are you mad?
YOU: No. I'm very happy eating a tofu burger. It's much better than McDonald's.
HER: See, I told you it's just like meat.
YOU (to yourself): Sort of like this relationship. It seems so real, only I'm starting to think it's not what I had in mind.

THE ONLY QUESTION THAT MATTERS

A man may say, "Okay, I guess this is it." He may get married and have kids. But years down the line, none of it really matters unless he's made the most important decision.

Commitment . . . or New Pussy?

On one hand, there's commitment: You and your woman together, forever. Living, sharing, loving, growing. It's the most beautiful thing in the world, and in his heart of hearts a man knows that.

On the other hand there's New Pussy. This needs no explanation.

It's a tough decision because lots of men don't look at marriage as gaining a good woman, they look at it as giving up New Pussy.

Commitment or New Pussy?

Every man's got to decide.

Commitment will give you a headache every now and then.

New Pussy always clears your mind.

But in the long run, if you're sick, is New Pussy gonna take care of you?

No.

If you're hungry, is New Pussy gonna feed you?

New Pussy can't cook!

If you have a baby, is New Pussy gonna teach her to read?

New Pussy's illiterate!

Eventually you come back to Commitment and learn that the only way to make it work is the age-old trick: turn this Old Pussy into New Pussy. That's right. Recycle the pussy.

But how?

You gotta try new stuff, like having sex in places you haven't had sex before. Let's see: the car, the den sofa, and the hall closet are out. How about her ass? Even better, how about . . . at her mother's house . . . when her mother's there . . . on the kitchen table while her mother's eating? And make her watch. That'll keep the Old Pussy new. It might even get her mama interested, but that's another story. Just remember what you gotta do: make the Old Pussy new, because if it ain't new, it's through.

*   *   *

I don't need a woman to do *anything* in bed. I just need a woman who will *contemplate* doing anything in bed.

PHONE SEX

One way to keep it new is phone sex. This is perfect for when you're on the road, or in the office, or even on the other line in the next room.

So you make a call . . . and hope for the best.

I don't know, I just don't feel comfortable with this, Chris.

Oh come on, come on. So what do you have on?

Underwear.

Come on, don't say 'underwear.' Say panties. Little panties, right? What kind of panties?

Um, like a tweed, Lycra blend.

Oh come on, what am I, a tailor? Come on, what's the cut? What panties; a G-string? A thong? Come on, come on. Okay, do you miss me?

Yeah.

What you going to do when you see me?

Um . . . I don't know. Talk. Hold you.

You want me to hold you back?

Yeah.

You want me to kiss you?

Um, I guess so.

You want me to eat your pussy?

Ah, whatever.

What do you mean, whatever? Do you want me to eat your pussy?

Eventually, I guess . . . it'll get there, I mean, yeah. I mean, I don't know.

Could you just say it, if you want it, say it.

All right, um . . .

Do you want me to eat your pussy?

I would like it if you ate my . . .

Ate your what?

My . . . ussy, ah hem . . .

Excuse me? Your russy? What? If I ate your what?

My pussy.

Okay, okay. What you going to do to me?

Touch your arm.

What the fuck you want to touch my arm for?

Well, you know, I'll rub it.

You'll rub my arm?

Uh huh.

What the fuck. I ain't in a fight, I didn't fall down.

All right, I'll massage your neck.

You got to go lower.

Um, I'll kiss your ear.

Eh, eh, eh, you got to go lower than that.

What if I rub your tummy?

Lower. Lower.

All right. I'll touch your pen . . . penis.

My penis?

Uh hum.

My penis?!

Uh hum.

What the fuck you talking about—penis? What the fuck penis?
Penis? What's this penis shit? It's dick. Dick. My dick! What am I,
a fucking doctor?

Good phone sex is great. But there's nothing worse than
bad phone sex.

i DO, i THiNK

Once upon a time I thought that if it was left up to me, my wedding-day festivities would fall between breakfast and the Sunday afternoon basketball game.

And I wouldn't have any of that traditional stuff.

My bride and I would glide up to the altar wearing long, white fur coats and Rollerblades. I'd pull the plug on the organ and bring in DJ Grandmaster Flash. We'd do the Electric Slide right there in the church with the Reverend Little Richard performing the ceremony. I think he's a reverend. I hope so. And I wouldn't divide the seating arrangements by bride and groom. I would separate guests into the people who think we're doing the right thing, and the people who think we're ruining our lives. That way, if I ever got divorced, I'd know who to call.

After you've tied the knot, the truth about each other finally comes out.

When you were still dating, the person who wanted marriage the most would only argue so much. If it was the woman, she wasn't going to bitch too loud when you didn't pick up your dirty socks, or when you let dishes pile up in the sink. That might have blown her deal.

Once you got married, though, she's got it saved up: all the yelling, all the complaining.

> HER: Remember how I said I find it annoying when you leave your clothes around?
> YOU: Yeah?
> HER: Well, I fucking *hate it* when you leave your clothes around.
> YOU: But—
> HER: And remember when I said I'd like you to wash the dishes sometimes?

YOU: Yeah.

HER: Muthafucka, wash those dishes *now!*

ONE iS NEVER ENOUGH

Men are always complaining: "How come I get only one wife? I want another wife. What man wouldn't?" You have visions of harems dancing in your head.

But, you know, I'd be willing to give up that little fantasy if . . . my wife could have another husband—or two.

This is how it would work: one husband would be normal; in other words, me. The other would be one of those platonic friends who are always hanging around. I wouldn't even have to approve of him. It could be her choice. And all he has to do is take her to the shit I don't want to go to.

Like the Ice Capades. I don't want to watch somebody skate! I don't give a fuck about Nancy Kerrigan or Brian Boitano.

HER: Do it for me.

ME. Hell, no. I'm not sitting though ice skating!

I might go see Tonya Harding, though, but only because she's got the slut factor and a nice ass.

I also don't want to go to her girlfriend's wedding. Boring. I'd be miserable there. There'd be nothing fit to eat. And she'd be mad that I'm not talking to anyone.

HER: You're so quiet.

ME: What am I supposed to say? I don't know these people.

HER: Yes, you do. They're my friends.

ME: I hate your friends.

Here's what I really want to say: **"Take your other husband!"**

No. I'm not going to take you to *The English Patient.* Get your other husband to do that.

Evita? No. Take the other guy. I want to watch the fucking game.

No, I don't want to go shopping with you. It takes you two hours just to pick out a shirt.

Yoga? Call a girlfriend. Even I wouldn't ask your other husband to do that shit.

One wedding I wouldn't mind going to is when my wife marries her other husband. Happiest day of my life. Just hurry up and do it so I don't have to keep doing all this other shit.

The "other husband" type is not gay. But he's damn near. He likes to do what women like to do. And he *cares*. He really cares. I care only to appease my woman. *He's* the friend. He's really excited when our wife opens up the paper and shows him Kathie Lee Gifford's new house. Who gives a fuck about that? Or Princess Diana's newest dress. Do I care about the royal family? I don't give a flying fuck. I'm not mad at them or anything, it's just a nonfactor in my life.

HER:	Di's so beautiful.
OTHER HUSBAND:	Yes. Look at her. How does she do it?
ME:	No, she's not. She's an average-looking woman. In the real world they wouldn't even let Princess Di point at a can opener on "The Price Is Right."

The weird thing is that eventually the second husband is the guy your wife will end up with after she's tired of your shit. You're the guy she's fucking and he's the guy she should be fucking. Come to think of it, women *always* have two men in their lives, and sometimes three: the guy she's fucking, the guy she should be fucking, and the guy she wants to fuck. Lots of guys reading this right now don't know who they are.

Am I right?

Who are you?

The other husband comes in handy especially when you don't want to have sex with your wife. (Yeah, he can have sex with her, but not all the time. Husband number one has certain rights.)

When *she* doesn't want to have sex there's no use making a big deal about it.

You want it.

Can't have it.

Better get used to it. No means no. There's no bad reason for a woman to turn down sex.

> **HER:** Just got my hair done and it hurts.
>
> We did it two weeks ago.
>
> My pussy's going to explode! There. You made me tell you.
>
> Are you happy now?

But the three times a year that you're not interested, it's a catastrophe. Women can turn you down 30 times a month but if you say no, it's:

"What? Who are you fucking? You fucking someone at your job? How dare you?"

The ironic part is that she didn't really want to have sex in the first place because she was so turned on by you. You were real busy doing something else and she just wanted to see if she could get you away from that. Or she noticed another woman looking at you.

* * *

Before you lived together you fucked all the time. Before, she had to think, "I don't know how long he's going to be here and I want him to come back."

Once you got married there's no more anticipation about you coming over. You're *always* over. Now you have to come back . . . *because you live there!*

Before marriage, it was all about your woman trying for the ring. She had to have that ring. That's what all the sex everywhere in the city was about. It had nothing to do with her being hot. She'd do anything for the ring.

Now women suddenly have an official rule book about how to get a man.

Here's what I want to know: is there a chapter in *The Rules* about blowing a guy while he's driving? Where's that chapter? You want the ring . . . ?

KEEP iT iN YOUR PANTS

Monogamy is rough. Very few animal species even bother with it—just penguins and some rare African butterfly. I can understand why: all penguins do is stand around together on the ice. If a male cheats it can't go unnoticed, and there's a good chance he'll be a seal snack by dinnertime. As for the butterfly, it's easy to be monogamous if you're that tough to catch.

Humans aren't too good at monogamy.

Make that male humans.

Here's the bottom line: once you commit, you can't cheat.

Wanna cheat.

Can't cheat.

Dying to cheat.

Can't cheat.

Can't *wait* to cheat.

Can't cheat.

Some folks gotta go to rehab not to cheat.

Some folks cheat in rehab.

Here's why you can't cheat: your woman will lose her mind and in some cases she will actually try to kill you.

Not cheating is hard. No one said it was easy. But your woman doesn't want to hear about your pain. She has no time for your complaining. She wants to hear that she's the only woman in your life. No, she wants to hear that she's the only woman in your life and that the sight of all other women makes you want to vomit.

That's nice. But it's still hard not to cheat. Why? Because lots of single women *like* men who are in relationships. Desperation is the worst cologne, and guys who are in good relationships never seem hungry. Nothing gets men more attention than not needing it—except not wanting it. Guys know what I'm talking about. When you're single nobody's thinking about your ugly ass. But then a woman gets hold of you, washes you down, gives you a Breathsaver, and wipes all the crust out of your eyes, suddenly every woman you meet wants what you've got and, until recently, couldn't give away for free.

When you were single nobody called up. Now your office phone rings off the hook. You got those crazy, freaky sex calls like, "Hey, whatcha doin'? Me and my girlfriend are having a dick-sucking contest, and we thought you'd be a good judge." Never got that call when you were single, did you? Now you get it every Tuesday. And you never even met these women.

Still can't cheat. Why? You're gonna get *caught.*

I don't care who you are. You could be 007.

You're gonna get caught.

Believe me, you don't want to get caught. I'd rather be caught stealing nuclear secrets from the government than to be caught cheating on a woman.

I got caught once. Once. I remember it like it was yesterday. A woman found two condoms in my pocket. That was very bad. Very bad. Real bad.

It was a pack of three.

HER: Where's the other condom? Where's the *other* condom? Where the *fuck's* the other condom? **Where's the other condom?**

This is when you make an important discovery: women are like the police. They can have all the evidence in the world, but they still want the confession.

HER: I know you did it. Just admit it. I know you did it, just admit it.
YOU: Didn't do it.
HER: I got it on film. I know you did it, just admit it.
YOU: Didn't do it.
HER: Can't you be a man? Can't you be a *fuck'n* man? **I *know* you did it, just admit it.**
YOU: Wasn't me.
     (Men: This *is* the proper response. Even if she catches you together *in bed*, deny it was you. Sometimes it works.)

If hammering at you fails, a woman will get psychological. She'll try to trick you into confessing.

HER: It'll be all right if you just say you did it. It'll be all right, if you just say you did it. Honey . . . it'll be all right, if you just say you did it.

You hear that nine hundred times and you start losing your mind. You start thinking, *I guess it'll be all right if I just say I did it.*

YOU: Honey, I did it. Will it be all right?

HER: **No, it ain't all right! I can't believe you did that!**

YOU: But I thought you said you knew?

HER: I didn't know until you told me.

A man is only as faithful as his options.

Some guys don't fuck around because they just don't. Other guys know they won't be able to see their kids. Other guys can't bear the thought of paying half the mortgage *and* rent at the same time. But for most of us it's much simpler: who's got the time to fuck around?

Lots of guys never even thought about cheating until their mate got jealous about something innocent. That put the idea into his head: "Why am I going through all this pain without any gain? It just doesn't make sense."

I'm never jealous. In my profession that would be insane. I'm never home. If I thought about who my woman might be with I'd lose my mind.

For all I know, she's getting fucked right now.

If she finds out you were cheating and she wants to break up, here's what you do:

RUN!

You got off lucky.

RUN!

If you move too slowly toward the door you won't get that lucky. She'll call out and say, "Wait, let's work it out." But "work it out" really means "payback."

You know what payback is? It means you can stay in the house, sleep in the same bed, watch her get dressed in the morning and undressed in the evening, but you're not getting pussy for a *long* time. You're not getting pussy until the Bills win the Superbowl.

And she's going to make sure you're not getting any new

pussy either. She'll get you a beeper, a cellular phone, a car phone. Every time you're outside you'll have to check in:

"I'm outside, I'm in the car, I'm on the road, I'm at the supermarket, I bought a pack of franks, I got some butter, I'm coming home, I'm on my way, I ran a light, the cops are chasing me, they're chasing me, they're chasing me, they're chasing me, I ran out of the car, they shot me in the leg, I'm a' hopping, I'm a' hopping, I'm almost home, I'm almost home, I'm in the driveway, I'm right next to you, I LOVE YOU."

Eventually your woman might forgive you. But she'll never forget. You'll be driving to Grandma's house, and you'll say, "Do I make a right turn here?"

She'll say, "Did you make a right turn with that *bitch*? From now on, no matter where we go, it's all left turns, do you understand?"

But you know what? If you stay together, eventually she'll start to trust you again. Then a crazy thing happens. *You* stop trusting *her*. You cheated on her and now you don't trust her. Strange but true. You know why?

Because you gave her a **"get-dick-for-free card."**

And you never know when she's gonna cash it in.

A LiTTLE PORNO

Everyone lies in a relationship. Everyone has secrets. We can't go into all of them here, but for men it's that most have some porno hidden in their house.

You know it's true. I can feel your tension already. You're squeezing the pages together really hard. (Hey, motherfucker. Let up!)

The porno is tucked away for those trying times. It's not a lot, not an illegal amount. It's just enough to get you by. It helps keep the nasty-taboo element alive. A man figures, "I may not be having kinky, freaky sex, but I'm glad to know *somebody* is."

When men hide their porno stuff, they really hide it. A man becomes Batman. It's not behind the speaker, not behind the dresser, not under the couch. You pull at a book on the bookcase, the whole fucking wall slides to the left, and you descend two flights of stairs into The Porno Pit.

"Free at last!"

But you know what? One day your woman's going to find the porno. It won't be because she moved the book that led to your hiding place. Nothing like that.

You'll just **leave it out.**

Your woman will leave for work early one morning. You'll go down into The Pit and get a tape for a little look. Just a jerk before work. But you'll lose track of time. "Oh shit, this is getting good. Oh shit, what time is it? I got to get to work."

Then you'll rush off and leave the tape in the VCR.

It's just negligence.

Later, your woman and her girlfriend come home and decide to watch "The Nanny." They turn on the TV and it's a "Very Special Nanny." Only the nanny they remember never wore crotchless panties or screamed for a naked policeman to spank her ass. Now your woman's embarrassed in front of her girlfriend. They can only watch for fifteen, twenty minutes before they're so shocked they just have to turn it off.

Hours pass. Your woman broods and waits for you to come home. She's got your porno tape in her hand. She's got a tear in her eye. She doesn't know what's going on, but she feels like you cheated on her with a tape. She's hurt and beat down. When you walk in the door, she's waiting.

YOU: Wassup, baby?

HER (shaking the tape, screaming): Is this what you like? Is this what the fuck you like? Is it? Is this what gets you off? Is this what the fuck you like?

So you've got to lie and go, "No."

Meanwhile, you're thinking, "Of course that's what I like. I built an underground cavern for it, didn't I? It's a regular *Shawshank Redemption* down there."

She keeps going. "I see there's two women in there having sex. Is that what you like? Is that what you want? Do you want me to have sex with my girlfriend Michelle, while you watch?"

You'll just smile, but you'll be thinking, "Michelle? Oh shit, I never even thought of that one. Why did you even put that in my head, woman? Now every time I see Michelle I'll have to leave the room."

She still won't stop. "Is that what you like? Tell me now if it is so I can pack up and go."

And maybe she should go, because a relationship is pretty much over when you can't share the things you like. That's when you stop showing her parts of yourself. For a relationship to last and stay satisfying, you have to be able to tell her, "I love you, I'll always take care of the kids—and sometimes I watch a little porno."

YAKETY YAK, DON'T TALK BACK

Relationships. Easy to get into, too hard to maintain.

At first you can't stop talking, but at some point you quit

because you have heard *everything* this person has to say. And it makes you sick to your stomach.

HER: Remember that time—
YOU: Yeah, I remember that time.
HER: Ever tell you about the time—?
YOU: Yeah, you told me. Stop telling me. Why don't you go out and get kidnapped and have some new shit happen to you?

It's sad.

Women love to talk. If there was talking in the Olympics, a man wouldn't stand a chance. The problem is that *women want to talk to you.* They want to talk to their *man.* But they don't want to "talk" talk. They just want you to "listen" listen. All a woman needs is to be asked the correct question that will allow her to run her mouth. They want you to set 'em up. It's a comedy team and you're the straight man.

Here's how to make your woman happy: all you have to do is say, "How was your day?"

It's a 45-minute conversation.

You don't have to talk. You just have to *act* like you're talking.

"Uh huh."

"Get outta here."

"You don't say?"

"That ain't right."

"I tol' you that bitch crazy."

You have to say, "I tol' you that bitch crazy," because every woman has another woman at work that she cannot stand. And every woman exaggerates the problem and makes it into some sort of "Dynasty" bullshit.

HER: She's trying to *destroy* me.
YOU: What do you mean, "destroy?" You wrap bags at JC Penney. What are you talking about? Is the woman ripping your paper? Come on!

Men have to know when to listen. Women, on the other hand, have to learn when *not* to talk. (That's not the same as listening.) It's not that men don't want to hear women talk, it's that they shouldn't talk so much *just as soon as we get home*. You ever notice that no man comes home straight from work? A man gets off work, he's got to go somewhere. He's got to drink something. He's got to smoke something. He's got to watch a game. He's got to hang out with his boys.

He's got to do something that'll get him mentally prepared for all the talking he's getting ready to hear.

We put a foot in the door and it's "You ain't gonna believe . . . blah, blah, blah."

We take another step, and it's "So I tol' that bitch . . . yak, yak, yak."

Let a man get situated. We don't need to hear it all right away. Let us get our other foot in the fucking door. Let us get something to drink. Let us get a ham sandwich. Let us take a shit!

POETRY iN COMMOTiON

Women don't like nice guys.

They say they do.

They don't.

They've got to be with an asshole first. They have to go with Ike, then Mike.

The problem is that if you're a nice guy you always get women after they've been out with the asshole. Now you get to be her boyfriend *and* her psychiatrist, to help her get over this crazy man. For every twenty minutes of pussy there's three hours of therapy.

It starts in childhood. Little girls like little bad boys.

If a little boy gives a little girl a Valentine's Day card, she doesn't want anything to do with him. She wants the little boy who just punched her in the back and ran down the hall.

"Oh I luv him . . . he cute."

Then you grow up and you marry that same little boy. Next thing you know, you're on "Ricki Lake," nursing a black eye and adjusting your new dentures, going, "I don't know what I did to deserve this. It just ain't right."

You don't? You *picked* that man. You *chose* him. You could have had Nice Boy Roy but instead you wanted Asswhip McGee.

YOU: But, Ricki, I *love* Asswhip. Between beatings he writes poetry.

RICKI: Did you bring some?

YOU: I did. "Violets are blue, roses are red, time to kick the bitch in the head." It's an Asswhip McGee original.

You know who I feel sorry for more than anybody else?

Ike Turner.

Ike was the king of woman beaters until O.J. took his title. Now, Ike's going, "Hey, I *coulda* killed Tina. What about me? What's blood got to do with it?"

You know that rule book for women about how to get a man?

Ike Turner also wrote a "rules" book.

Rule one: Shut up.

Rule two: Never date a woman stronger than you.

Rule three: I said, shut up!

Rule four: Get in the first punch.

Rule five: I told you to shut the fuck up!

Everybody says there's *no reason ever* to hit a woman. And they're right.

But at the same time, nobody's above an ass-whipping.

BUT JUST DON'T DO IT.

Unfortunately, there's nothing more crazy, more out of control, more likely to embarrass you in a restaurant than a woman who knows you aren't going to hit her. When a woman is with a man she knows one hundred percent isn't going to strike her, she *can't wait* for him to do something wrong, so she can yell at him like he's a little boy.

> HER: What the fuck you gonna do? Kiss my ass. I don't care where we at, just kiss my punk ass. Fuck you, fuck you, fuck you!

Meanwhile, the poor man's smiling at the other diners, thinking, "How the fuck did I get into this situation?"

I'll tell you: your woman knew she could get away with it.

If I'm having an argument with a man who's bigger than I am, I know there's a zone I don't go into. I would never hit a man bigger than me. In a million fucking years. I know I can't hit a guy and get away with it.

Not women. Women will go at you. They don't give a fuck. They'll slap you, kick you, punch you, and spit on you.

> HER: What the fuck are you going to do?

Occasionally she'll say the wrong thing, like, "Your momma's a bitch." Then she knows she went too far and she braces herself for a smack. But if the hit doesn't come she's thinking, "Ooh, I got him now, the little-dick motherfucker." Then, she says, "I fucked all your friends."

And for good measure she hits *you*.

Let's be clear: Even if a woman hits you, I don't think it's cool to hit back. I've never hit a woman in my life. I never *would* hit a woman.

But I'd **shake the shit** out of one.

* * *

Of course, some guys don't get it. They hit. They kill. Then they deny it.

Look at O.J. People thought he was going to crack in the civil trial. He didn't. He didn't give a fuck. He's not afraid. He's been hit by Mean Joe Green. He's not scared of a lawyer. He had a new strategy. "You ain't seen it, I didn't do it. Did you see it? Well, I didn't do it."

Didn't do it? If you have one kid in the house and the cookie jar is broken and the kid has crumbs on his face, no matter what he says—*he did it!*

O.J. had crumbs up his ass!

But he was in total denial. He didn't care about the evidence. They had the blood, they had the shoes, they had the Bronco. But O.J. decided to hold on tight and ride the lie. He said, "Did you see it? Then I didn't do it."

It was hysterical.

"When's the last time you hit Nicole?"

"Who's Nicole?"

"The woman you killed."

"Someone's dead?"

THE END iS JUST BEGiNNiNG

Some people say that opposites attract.

We're already opposites. We're men and women. That's enough. You want to get something more opposite? A double opposite? You're asking for trouble.

You could find a woman born in the same neighborhood, on the same day, in the same year, went to the same schools, likes the same foods, hates the same movies—you're still opposites.

That's why whatever you're into, your woman's got to be into, and vice versa. You're Born Again, she's got to be Born Again. If you're a crackhead, your woman's got to be a crackhead.

> **YOU:** I'm going to Bible study, what are you doing?
> **HER:** Hitting the pipe.

Got to be into the same shit or it won't work out.

A relationship *could* be over when every conversation leads to an argument.

It's *probably* over when you *want* to argue, but you don't say anything because you're saving it up for next time. It's almost like you're preparing your case for your day in court. Here are some good things to save up:

- She didn't tell you her family was coming to visit.

- She spent more on a Gucci belt than a couch. Twice.

But you have to be careful. You can't be hasty. You need to take your time, build your case, and collect all the evidence you need to justify your exit.

A relationship is *definitely* over when you don't even *try* to fuck. When a man comes home and says, "I'm going to go to bed," and doesn't even fight for it anymore, it's over. If you're still having sex you'll find a way to handle all your other problems, no matter what they are. You will work it out.

If you're fucking.

She's a little bit country, he's a little bit rock and roll. But we're fucking.

We're fine.

* * *

Man and woman do not live by broccoli and cheese alone. There's got to be more on the plate. And the plate's got to be good and strong itself. This is why smart people say you gotta think about life in the long term. Dumb people tell you life is short.

No, it's not.

Life is long.

Especially if you make the wrong choices.

SOCIAL STUDIES

Why do black leaders always say such ignorant shit?

"We got to stop this black-on-black crime."

There's no such thing as black-on-black crime.

It's just crime. Everybody robs their own people. Nobody goes someplace else to rob people. When you say black-on-black crime, you know what you're really saying? Crime is cool if you rob white people.

There's no black-on-black crime. It's broke-on-broke crime. A bunch of broke people robbing each other.

"I only got four dollars. Give me your three!"

I was watching Geraldo's show, "Live from Death Row." He spent two hours with psychos—none of them black men. Black crime tends to be stupid, not crazy. When you hear on the news that somebody chopped off his girlfriend's head, drank her blood, and used her toes to play pool, chances are it was a white guy.

Find an old lady kicked down the stairs for her welfare check? A black guy did it.

Someone cut out the old lady's eyes and used them as knick-knacks? Definitely a white guy.

Every night people watch the news, hear a crime story, and wait for the videotape to see the alleged criminal's color. White people watch the story and say, "Betcha it was a black guy." Black people watch the story and say, "Please, Lord, don't let it be a black guy. I want to go to work tomorrow in peace."

BASKETBALL JONES

A guy on the radio the other day was saying, "We need after-school centers because the kids don't have a place to go play ball. And that's when bad things happen."

What ever happened to just being bored? When I was a kid we were just plain bored. And we didn't shoot anybody. Can't kids be bored anymore?

No, they need sports.

Look: if a basketball is the only thing that will stop you from killing somebody, then I don't want you to play ball. I want you off the streets. I'm not ready to hear, "Good thing I got this ball. If I ain't had this, boy, I'd be blowing some motherfucker's head off right now."

Now, midnight basketball is the hot thing.

"We've got to offer midnight basketball or there's going to be some *crime*."

What happened to getting some sleep so you could go look for a job in the morning? What about *that* program?

"I missed the job interview—but I scored forty-five!"

THE AMERiCAN PRiSON EXPERiENCE

Before I joke about prisons, let me say I understand that there are people in there for socioeconomic reasons. And I understand that there are people in there who didn't do it.

And I feel for you. I really do.

But if you actually did it, *fuck you.*

I keep reading about how outraged the people are at our overcrowded prisons. It doesn't make any sense. I thought that was the whole idea of prison: a place for prisoners to feel uncomfortable. My house is a little crowded, but we never burnt a mattress, went on a hunger strike, or took my mother hostage.

The problem isn't overcrowding. The problem is repeat offenders. We need to make jails tougher. We need to create an American Prison Experience. Something no one will forget. Maybe we can get one of the movie studio theme parks in on it.

Make it a ride.

I know it will work.

Only in America do we have this problem of repeat offenders.

Look at Russia: no one goes to Siberia twice.

They don't have this problem in Iran. It's really hard to snatch another purse when you're missing a hand. And it's really tough to lie to the judge when you have no tongue.

We're way too nice to criminals in the United States. Criminals get three meals a day. Homeless people get nothing. Prisoners should get one meal a day—dinner—but not like normal people. Just put a cow in the courtyard and see what happens. If you miss a meal, go to death row and get the extra meat off the electric chair.

When you're sentenced to death, we have lots of ways to kill you. Hanging, injection, firing squad, electric chair. I hate the electric chair.

Not because its inhumane.

Electricity simply costs too much money. Taxpayers' money. Your money. My $50.

There's got to be cheaper ways to kill people. How about a stabbing chair? Just strap the condemned man into a nicely padded recliner, let him lay back, and just when he's getting comfortable—a bunch of knives pop out all over. And if that doesn't kill him, bring out Nell Carter to sit on his head.

WE DON'T NEED JAiLS. WE GOT THE TOSSED SALAD MAN

Everyone's complaining.

"Jails aren't tough enough."

"We got to have the death penalty."

Don't believe the hype. Jails are fucked up because life is fucked up, too. People are broke, people are starving. Life's catching up to jail. If you live in an old project, life in a new jail isn't that bad.

HBO once aired a special about life in jail. Normally, jail

specials are on regular TV and there's lots of shit they don't show.

Not HBO. *They showed it all.*

They interviewed a brother. They asked him a reasonable and revealing question:

> **HBO:** When a new prisoner comes in, how do you initiate him?
>
> **INMATE:** The first thing I do is make him toss my salad.
>
> **HBO:** Toss your salad? What's that?
>
> **INMATE:** Havin' your salad tossed means havin' your asshole eaten out with jelly or syrup. I prefer syrup.

I am not making this up.

> **HBO:** Wh-wh-why must you go through all of that, sir? Why not just oral sex?
>
> **INMATE:** Well, when a man's sucking your dick, he can pretend it's something else. When he's eating ass he *knows* it's ass.

We don't need a death penalty. We've got the Tossed Salad Man. If I had the choice between the electric chair and tossing a salad I'd be like, "So where do you plug it in? Shouldn't I be wet first?"

Everybody's talking about public education being out of control.

"We need tougher rules. We need prayer in the schools."

We don't need that shit. We just need the Tossed Salad Man. He'd straighten out those kids.

> **TEACHER:** Hey, Jimmy, you got a D. You know what you've got to do.
>
> **JIMMY:** NOOOOO!!!! NOOOO!! I don't wanna toss a salad, I don't wanna toss a salad. I'm gonna read!!! I'm gonna *learn* to read!!!

Being arrested is embarrassing enough, but the humiliation of being processed after the arrest is worse.

They make you strip naked, lift up your balls, and spread your ass cheeks. (Or so I'm told . . .) They want to make sure that you don't smuggle a lethal weapon into jail, in your ass.

I know. You're saying, come on, who's going to do something like that? But think about it. For someone to make that rule, it means someone else must have given them good reason. Whatever the guy who got caught with something in his ass had, it must have been pretty deadly for everyone to get their ass checked forevermore.

GUARD: What you got in there? Huh?

SUSPECT: All right, you got me. It's a gun. Help me get it out, okay? It'll makes my ass look too big in these prison pants, anyway.

There's no such thing as rehabilitation in jail. You know what criminals do in jail? They just go over and over the crime. They've got years to figure out where they went wrong. They make diagrams. Then a bunch of them sit around and discuss it.

INMATE #1: Okay. You robbed a bank, you ran outside. Which way did you go?

INMATE #2: I went left.

INMATE #1: Oh. That's where you fucked up, man. That's where you fucked up. If you'da went right you'd be a free man right now. When you get out of here, I want you to go right, okay?

Prison has its good points, though. For instance, child molesters always get treated like shit. They get spit and pissed on, and maybe eventually killed. An ax murderer will walk up to a child molester and say, "You know what? I'm gonna kill you."

"But why?"

"Because *you* have a serious problem."

MY HEROES

Everyone's got their favorite criminals. Mine are pimps.

We can all rob a bank, we can all sell drugs. Being a pimp is a whole other thing.

Why? Pimps have it all together. They do real well with women. You never see two pimps at a party and one pimp saying, "Go over there and talk to her. I think she likes you."

Pimps are cool for so many reasons.

Here's the big one:

A pimp can get a woman to sell her body and give him the money!

That's not a crime. That's a gift. That's a super power.

But how do they do it? What do pimps say?

Is it a magic word? Is it voodoo? Do they have a little watch that they swing in front of a woman's face while they say, "Okay, you be like a whore now."

What do pimps say?

We know more about aardvarks and wildebeests than pimps. Our government spends millions on research. We send people into space. We're cloning now. I don't give a fuck about cloning.

Tell me what pimps say!

How nice does a restaurant have to be when you ask a woman to go sell her body? How nice are the flowers you give her that day? What the fuck does a pimp say? How do they get away with that shit? An average man would get his ass whupped to even suggest such a thing. But a pimp is way beyond that. A pimp isn't an average man.

How does a pimp do it?

"You looking good, you lookin' real good. I got to ask you something. No, no, finish your soup. Damn, you looking good. You're fucking fine. You're a *fine*-looking woman.

"You remember when I said I'd do anything for you? I meant that. I meant that from the bottom of my heart. I'd do *anything*. I'd move a mountain for you. Do anything. But the question is, now . . . would you do *anything* for me?

"That other day when we was making love, I said to myself, 'Goddamn, this is good. This is the best loving I've ever had in my life. The best.' I know. I was in there, I had a lot. And all I could think was, 'You know what? The world needs some of this. We got wars all over the place, people are hungry. I think the world would be a better place if they just got a sample of this pussy. Everyone should be able to experience the love I'm feeling right now.'

"Baby, I think it's a shame to keep it to yourself. I don't want to be stingy. What if Colonel Sanders had kept the recipe to himself? Wouldn't be right, would it? No. Millions of people deprived of some good chicken. Well, I think your love is the same thing.

"So I need you go out there and do this for me. I would never want you to be on welfare. We respect ourselves. That's right. I want you to go out there, I want you to put on this miniskirt.

"Leave the panties here.

"And here's what I want you to do: I want you to sell your ass. I'll be in the car waiting."

You know what else I love about pimps? They don't change. The same pimp who was out on the street in 1972 is out there right now.

I'd like to know where he found that lizard jumpsuit. In green. You can't get a green lizard jumpsuit anywhere that I know. There must be a pimp boutique somewhere in New York.

FOR PiMPS ONLY!

When I was a kid I had an uncle who was a pimp. But I didn't know it. All I remember is my uncle Clay coming in at six or seven in the morning, with my aunt Samantha. Clay with a big hat and Samantha wearing a lot of makeup. But I was a kid, playing around, and I didn't think anything of it.

Now, when I look at old pictures, I know.

"This pimp was in our house. Aunt Samantha was a ho!"

What a great life.

MARiON BARRY, CRACKHEAD

I don't know where you're from, but where *I* come from the last thing you want is for a crackhead to be in charge of anything. That's why I was tripping when I saw the Million Man March. All the black leaders were there. Minister Farrakhan, Reverend Jackson, Mayor Marion Barry . . .

Marion Barry?! At the Million Man March? I know he's the mayor of Washington, D.C., but how did he get a ticket?

I thought it was supposed to be a day of pos-i-tiv-i-ty.

Marion Barry at the Million Man March. Do you know what that means? Even in our finest hour we had a crackhead on stage.

How the hell did Marion Barry get his job back?

I'll tell you: smoked crack, got his job back.

If you get caught smoking crack at McDonald's you're not going to get your job back. They can't trust you around the Happy Meals. They'll send your ass to Hardee's. But Marion Barry smoked crack and got his job back.

All I want to know is, who ran against him that was so bad that they lost to a crackhead?

Someone on heroin?

"Vote for me. Vote for me. Don't vote for crack, vote for smack."

How did Marion Barry get elected? How are you going to tell kids not to get high when their mayor's on crack?

"Don't get high. You won't be *nothing*."

"Oh yeah? I could be mayor!"

How do you spend tens of thousands of dollars on radio and TV ads and campaign literature, have the moral upper hand, and still lose to a man who smoked crack on national television?

Here's a list of the people I think should have been able to beat Marion Barry in an election:

Gomer Pyle

Arnold Horshack (or anyone on "Welcome Back Kotter")

Pinky Tuscadero

Rosa Lopez

Punxsutawney Phil

Marion Barry got mad at me for saying that. He told me I disrespected the good people of Washington, D.C., at a time when they were trying to get funding.

I felt his pain. So I lied and said I was sorry.

The man not only got caught smoking crack on camera, but cheating on his wife at the same time. And when he got busted, the first words out of his mouth were, "The bitch set me up!"

And this man got elected mayor *again*!

This just proves what I always say about black people: *We are the nicest people on earth*. Any other race would have had him killed.

I figure the mayoral election must have been decided during the debates. So I got the transcript. Here's an excerpt:

MODERATOR: Ladies and gentleman, welcome to Constitution Hall for the first in a series of mayoral debates leading up to the election. Tonight we have the Democratic candidates.

To my right, we have Sharon Pratt Kelly, the current mayor of the District of Columbia. And to my left, Marion Barry, the former mayor and current mayoral hopeful.

I must caution you. There will be NO VIDEOTAPING! The first questions will be posed by Richard Bates of the *George Washington Journal*.

RB: Thank you. My question is for Mr. Barry: how do you propose to make the school system better?

MB: Well, um, that's a good question. I intend to create and finance programs that increase community and parent involvement. I think teachers, parents, and the P.T.A. must work together to give children the support they need.

RB: And Ms. Kelly?

SPK: Well, the first thing I'm going to do is to discourage kids from smoking crack. Unlike my opponent here, Count Cracula, when I raise the money for after-school programs, you can believe it's not going to end up in a glass pipe.

MODERATOR: The next question is from Elia Rodriguez of the *Arlington Record*.

ER: Mr. Barry, how do you propose to bring down the spiraling crime rate?

MB: First thing I'm going to do is have a curfew, requiring all minors to be indoors by eleven p.m. In terms of criminal offenses, I'll institute stricter penalties for repeat offenders.

ER: Ms. Kelly?

SPK: Stricter penalties? What are you going to do, handcuff yourself? If we had stricter penalties, you wouldn't even be here right now.

Can somebody tell me why I'm losing to this crackhead? I work hard, lead a good life, I'm educated, I play by the rules, and what happens? The race is between me and a crackhead.

And you know what? I'm not standing for it. I refuse to stand up here with a damn crackhead. You want to vote for him, vote for him. But turn your back and he'll be selling the Washington Monument for ten dollars. I'm getting out of here. Good-bye.

MB: Now as you see, Ms. Kelly just left. That's one thing I can say to the good people of Washington. I'll never leave you. Now, if we're finished here, I'd like to invite everybody out for a drink.

THE CLINTON LEGACY

Nineteen ninety-six was a big election year. We got Clinton back. Clinton II.

It's not because the people necessarily *liked* Clinton. They just didn't want Dole to win. Even the people who wanted Clinton to lose didn't want Dole to win.

Dole's too old.

Dole was old to old people. Look at his hand—it's all fucked up. He can't save anybody. You saw *Independence Day:* the president's got to get in there and fly a spaceship. Dole can't do that.

Dole lost big-time. He got his ass whipped. No matter what

Clinton did, Dole couldn't fuck with him. Clinton could have shown up with a little black kid.

"This is my daughter, Makumbe."

Dole still would have lost.

At the end Dole was even trying to give away money.

DOLE: I'm going to cut taxes fifteen percent.

THE PEOPLE: No thanks. Just lower 'em at your house.

DOLE: But I'm giving away money.

THE PEOPLE: No, that's okay. Thanks, anyway.

I like Clinton. I don't think he's going to do anything for black people, but I don't think he'll go out of his way to fuck with us. That won't be his priority.

I also like Clinton because he really needs the job. He needs the money. Why? Clinton's got real problems. He doesn't have president problems. He's got *real* problems just like you and me:

He's running out of money.

His wife's a pain in the ass.

All of his friends are going to jail.

I can relate to Clinton.

I know Clinton.

I *am* Clinton.

Clinton gets too much flack. Every move he makes, his enemies are right up his ass. If Clinton spent a hundred-dollar bill, someone would put it up to the light.

It's almost as if we have a black president.

Leave him alone. He's president. Let him do what he wants to do. So what if he has people staying at his house? It's *his* house. The White House is his shit. He could paint it green, let the grass die, put in some cheap-ass wood paneling. It's his house. If I could get some money for letting people stay at my house, I damn sure would. I know if I stay at my mother's house I have to at least pay the phone bill.

Remember the time he got a haircut for $300? Everybody got all mad. "How dare he get a haircut for three hundred dollars?" I'm not mad—but I do want to meet the man who had the nerve to charge the president for a haircut. Who the fuck do you think you are?

If I was the president I wouldn't pay for shit. Ask me for $300 and I'll blow up your house.

i DiDN'T MEAN TO TURN YOU ON

Everyone's always on Clinton. Always on him.

Leave him alone.

Now they're trying to get him for sexual harassment. What happened? The girl came to his hotel room, he whipped it out, she said no, and left.

And she wants to sue *him?*

He's the one who got turned down.

What is sexual harassment anyway? What's the difference between sexual harassment and just being an asshole? You can't be an asshole no more?

I'll tell you what sexual harassment is: if the man is your boss and says "Fuck me or you're fired," *that's* sexual harassment. You go to jail. But that's the *only* thing that's sexual harassment. Everything else falls under: **just trying to get laid**.

You can't put a man in jail for trying to get laid. I don't care how ignorant he tries to get it, that's all he was trying to do. He did it because he *liked* you. There's a lot of pussy out there but he was trying to get *yours*.

Let's admit it. The problem is that it's all about looks.

Anita Hill started this; Anita Hill looking like Helen Willis from "The Jeffersons." If Clarence Thomas had looked like Denzel Washington, this shit would have *never* happened.

"Stop it, Clarence. You nasty—with your fine self."

So what's sexual harassment? When an ugly man tries to fuck you? "He's ugly. Call the police. Get the authorities. He don't look good."

Women need to cut that out. You're going to get old one day. Your titties are going to touch your knees, your ass is going to touch the ground, and you are going to wish you were being harassed.

If my daddy didn't harass my mother, I wouldn't be here.

i DiDN'T MEAN TO TURN YOU ON—ii

The other thing they're still trying to get Clinton on?

Gays in the military. Everybody got all mad. Don't let them in. Don't ask, don't tell.

Hey, if they want to fight, let them fight.

I'm not fighting.

I don't care if I see a Russian tank on I 95; I'm not doing anything.

I guess that makes *me* a faggot now.

THE ONCE AND FUTURE CLiNTON

So what's Clinton going to do when his second term is over?

Most ex-presidents are old. They build libraries. Lecture. Clinton will get a divorce. Get a boat. Have a party. The man's young. His future's ahead of him. He'll date models. Probably get a development gig at Universal Studios. Endorse a brand of condoms. Do some bit parts in movies and some guest-starring on TV. I see it now: "Tonight, a *very special* episode of 'Friends.' "

THE GREAT BLACK HYPE

Lots of black people thought General Colin Powell could have been president in 1996.

"He should run. He could win."

No, he couldn't. He had a better chance of winning a bronze medal in female gymnastics than of being the president of the United States. Why? White people wouldn't have voted for him.

They said they would, but they wouldn't. They said they would because it seemed like a cool thing to say. It's like when someone asks if you'll be an organ donor. It's cool to say yes. But when the time comes, forget it. What if they figure out a way to bring you back from the dead?

"Shit. I got no eyes. Ain't this a bitch. Back from the dead and I can't see shit. Mom, I'm back. Momma, where's my eyes?

You gave them to a little boy in Idaho? Now I've got to kill him to get my eyes back."

Colin Powell could never have been president. The best thing white people could ever say about him was, "He speaks so well. He is so well spoken."

"Speaks well" is not a compliment. It's what you say about retarded people who can barely talk. Why would people say that to Colin Powell? Did he have a stroke? He's a fucking educated man. What did people expect him to sound like?

"I'm gonna drop me a bomb to-day. I'll be Pres-O-Dent."

After Powell said no way, people started talking about him at least being vice president. They said he should do it for his country. Fuck the country. Why should he run with a guy he could beat? People only have the nerve to ask a black man to do something *that fucking stupid*. Would anyone ask Al Gore to run with Al Sharpton?

As long as you live, there will never be a black vice president—at least not while the president's white. People say, "Never say never." I'm saying never. You know why? Because some black guy will just kill the president.

I'd do it.

If we had a black vice president right now, I couldn't wait to kill the president. Why not? What's going to happen to me? I'll just be in jail with a bunch of black guys who are going to treat me like a hero for the rest of my life! Even if they had a death penalty—the black president would pardon me.

I'd be the biggest star in the history of jail. I'd be signing autographs. Guys in jail would come up to me saying, "Chris, Chris. Yo, Chris, man. I hope my kids turn out to be *just like you.*" Then they'd whisper in my ear, "You know I was getting ready to rape you until I realized who you was."

SQUEEZiNG THE LAST DROP OF JUiCE

O.J. Simpson got away with murder.

Black people were too happy.

White people were too mad.

White people said, "This is bullshit." I haven't seen white people that mad since they canceled "M*A*S*H." Meanwhile, black people said, "Yeah, we won. We won. We won."

What the fuck did we win? Every day I look in my mailbox for my O.J. prize.

Nothing.

Even after the trials, people still don't have it right. So let's break it down.

Ron Goldman *was* Nicole's boyfriend. Don't be mistaken about that. He wasn't just some guy returning sunglasses. When was the last time you left some shit in a restaurant and they brought it back to your house? You could leave a newborn baby in a restaurant and all they'd do is put him in the coat room.

Also, Ron was known to drive around town in a Ferrari that O.J. bought for Nicole. Think about this: I buy you a car. You let another man drive around in the car. My car. Are you out of your fucking mind? I don't even have a Ferrari, but if I saw someone driving my Pinto . . .

I'm not saying O.J. should have killed her.

But I understand.

Here's something else: O.J. was paying $25,000 a month in alimony. *Twenty-five thousand dollars.* What the fuck was she eating? I guess with that money she could afford to say, "I got to get some extra cheese on my Whopper."

I'm not saying O.J. should have killed her.

But I understand.

You can't expect somebody to give you a bunch of money and not feel like they have some say-so in your life. A guy like O.J. had never been rejected. He's good looking, great in sports, had a lot of money. He had success on every possible level. So of course he lost his mind when he found out his ex-woman was fucking a *waiter*.

I'm not saying O.J. should have killed her.

But I understand.

Nicole got divorced for a good reason. She thought O.J. was crazy. But it seems to me that if you think your man's crazy *you'd avoid the places he lives*. O.J.'s in L.A. Why was Nicole in L.A.? If a guy whips your ass and you divorce him, why do you move eight blocks away? Look what Tina Turner did. Ike's in Mississippi, Tina's in Finland. If Ike went to Europe, Tina'd go to Pluto.

Women have it too good. When they divorce they have it made. They go to court and start talking shit:

"Your Honor, I'm used to this, I'm used to that, I'm accustomed to this, I'm accustomed to that."

What does *accustomed* mean? What does that have to do with *anything?* You go to a restaurant you're *accustomed* to eating. When you leave, you're not eating anymore. They don't owe you a steak. Why do divorced men owe money to their ex-wives? It's over. Move along. Find some new man to tap out.

And what about what the man's used—I mean, *accustomed*—to? That might not be money, but during the course of a relationship, a man grows accustomed to a few things. I would love to see a man go to court and say, "Your Honor, check this out: I'm *accustomed* to fucking her four times a week. She can have the alimony, but I want some pussy payments."

I know why Nicole's dead. The alimony payments made

O.J. crack. She got the big-ass alimony; he ain't scored a touchdown in twenty years.

O.J. should have had a prenup. Everyone needs a prenup. If you've got twenty million dollars and your wife wants ten, big deal—you ain't starving. But if you make thirty thousand and your wife wants fifteen, you *might* have to kill her.

"I'm not going to move back in with my momma just because you don't love me anymore. You're gonna have to die."

Think about O.J.'s situation. Big alimony, another man driving around in his car and fucking his wife, and a house he's still paying the mortgage on.

I'm not saying he should have killed her.

But I understand.

Johnnie Cochran told us the O.J. case was all about race. It wasn't about race. It was about fame.

If O.J. wasn't famous he'd be in jail right now.

If O.J. drove a bus he wouldn't even be O.J. He'd be "Orenthal, the Bus Driving Murderer."

Everybody said, "Oh, the jury's so stupid." Not true. They knew what they had to do. If Jerry Seinfeld had been charged with a double murder, white people would have done the exact same thing. If the person who found the bloody glove just happened to be in the Nation of Islam, Jerry'd be a free man. He'd be eating his cereal right now.

OH NO! O.J. WiLL NEVER GO AWAY

O.J.'s part of the culture now. People who grew up in the sixties can find their place in history by remembering where they were when JFK, RFK, or MLK got shot.

Now people ask, "Where were you and what were you doing when the O.J. verdict came in?"

If that isn't bad enough, O.J. keeps talking. I hate that. You got away with murder. Just go away and shut up.

O.J.: But I can't earn any money. Let me make a living.

Well, you made a videotape saying you didn't do it—and expected people to buy it. If you wanted people to buy it, you should have made a tape saying you killed her. Show us how you did it.

O.J.: I was hiding in the bushes. I didn't breathe. Me and the bushes were one. Now, I didn't really mean to kill her. But when I got there, I looked in the window and she had the candles burning, like she was getting ready to fuck somebody.

That got me mad. She came out with the dog. I jumped out of the bushes. I said, "I was just coming over for the weekly beating. But now I can see you're getting ready to fuck someone else. How dare you?"

I had to kill her. I slit her throat, hacked her up, tried to cut the titties out. I figured, I paid for 'em. Shit!

I didn't plan on killing nobody else. One killing's enough. Besides, I had a plane to catch.

But then Ron Goldman came around. I didn't know who he was. Then he saw what happened to Nicole and he said, "Hey! What are you doing?"

I said, "Killing the ho. Care to join her?"

Afterward, I gave the clothes to A.C. and he hid them in Chicago. If you find the clothes, the knife, or the shoes, you win a prize. Johnnie, tell them what they win."

JOHNNIE COCHRAN: Certainly O.J. Find the clothes, a year's supply of Popeye's Fried Chicken. Find the shoes, vacation for two to Peru. Find the knife, O.J. will kill *your* wife.

People say that if O.J. had gone to prison, no one would have fucked with him. He's famous. He killed two people.

Right.

They've got people behind bars who *meant* to kill two people. If O.J. had gone to jail, some brother would have said, "Hey, O.J. Why don't you come over here and toss my salad? And put some juice on it."

The first O.J. trial was such a hit they brought him back for another.

O.J. II.

That was a cool trial. O.J. even got on the stand.

They found him liable.

But people still say they think he didn't do it.

He did. If he didn't, then Nicole's not dead.

Now O.J. has to pay 33.5 million dollars. Meanwhile, they're going to take everything he owns: his house, his clothes, his Heisman. Everything. Took the doorknobs yesterday. Taking the paint tomorrow.

It's so bad that O.J. may have to move back in with his mom.

But he can't.

They're going to take her house, too. That's some sick shit. But it's his own damn fault. O.J. put his mother's house in his name, as an asset. I don't know why he did it, but you've got to be smarter than that.

Everything I give my mother is worthless.

His mother probably said, "Orenthal. Please don't put my house in your name."

And he said, "Don't worry, Mom. It's safe. I'd have to kill my wife for them to get it. And everyone knows I'm not gonna do something silly like that."

Now he's got to pay the money, and then he's got to find a job. But what can he do?

Home Shopping Network. O.J.'s Cutlery Showcase.

Horror movies. Can you imagine anything scarier than O.J. chasing you with a knife? Yes. O.J. getting away with it.

Professional wrestling. He wouldn't even need a costume.

"Ladies and gentlemen. In this corner, O.J.!"

"Booooo!"

WAiT! WHAT iF O.J. DiDN'T DO iT?

If O.J. looked like Leon Spinx they would have said guilty in minutes. But O.J. had the "good-looking-man" factor going for him. Those middle-aged sisters on the jury came to court every day and stared at this good-looking man; a good-looking man they'd like to fuck. Then they started thinking about their fat, ugly husbands at home.

"Hmmm. Maybe O.J. didn't do it."

People ask me, "Chris. Do you think O.J.'s guilty or not?"

I *hope* he's guilty.

If not, then the whole damn country owes him one big apology. But how could we apologize?

We'd have to give him back his life.

Even worse, we'd have to let him back on "Monday Night Football."

Shit. I hope he's guilty.

The only way we'd find out he's not guilty is if there was some last-minute evidence—like a videotape. Every night you see amateur videotapes on the TV news. Every night. I don't get it. How is it that someone *just happens* to be hanging around—with a five-pound video camera—every time something happens? When Rodney King got his ass beat. When white cops rough up a black pedestrian. When an airplane crashes. How do they know in advance?

Suppose there was a tape of the murders and we could see that it's not O.J. coming out of Bundy Drive. Maybe it's Detective Vannatter, or Kato, or Walter Payton. Imagine that! Then we'd really have riots in the streets. There'd be wave after wave of black people going, "Told you so!"

Every black newspaper in the country. "Told you so!"

O.J.'s family going, "Told you so."

O.J. saying, "Lick my ass."

Imagine if he didn't do it. My God.

How could we make it up to O.J.?

Denise Brown would have to fuck him.

Her mother, too.

NOT
FROM
CONCENTRATE

When I was a kid I used to love O.J. Simpson. It was all about O.J. and Reggie Jackson, with a sprinkle of Joe Morgan. O.J. was the only football player I cared about. I did a book report on O.J. in the third grade, and every year I'd take that same book report, rewrite it, and hand it in for class.

I even had an O.J. football jersey. I knew everything about O.J. from reading that 90-page book that third graders could order from the *Weekly Reader*. I remember knowing that he had a fine wife and an Afro.

One of my fondest memories was when my father and I watched a Thanksgiving Day football game in which the Buffalo Bills played the Detroit Lions. It started with my dad saying, "He's good, but he ain't no Jim Brown." Then O.J. gained 275 yards and set a record. At the end my dad said, "That's the best running I've seen in my life." It was a bonding moment with me and Dad. O.J. brought us together.

I even met O.J. once at Kennedy Airport. He walked over and shook my hand. I called my brother Tony and told him all about it. It was like meeting a hero. O.J. was right up there with Eddie Murphy, Sugar Ray Leonard, and Bill Cosby.

I loved O.J.

It's a damn shame all of this happened.

THE CHOICE

I attended an abortion rally in D.C. I figured, what better place to pick up women. And you know they're fucking. It's not like you're going to meet a bunch of virgins at an abortion rally.

The abortion issue is all screwed up. You've got a Supreme Court mostly of men voting on abortion. But it's a women's issue.

We should have separate Supreme Courts: one for men, one for women. It's bad enough that a bunch of men get to vote on abortion. I wouldn't want a bunch of women voting on what I could do with my balls.

"The Supreme Court today ruled that two balls are too many."

Women should have the right to make the choice.

But what's the choice? It costs $5,000 to have a child and only $400 for an abortion. What kind of choice is that? Clearly, budget determines your choice.

Roe vs. *Wade* really means broke vs. paid.

So you look over your bills and make your choice.

"Are we gonna have Timmy or cable? I gotta catch the Tyson fight."

The crazy thing now is that abortion clinics advertise. It's so weird how they do it. They never say *abortion*, they say, "We terminate pregnancies." They say it as if they're giving the fetus a pink slip: "Hey, kid, you're fired."

But now that abortion clinics are advertising, you know what's next. Abortion sales on holidays. Come on down to the Lincoln's Birthday Abortion Sale. You know, Lincoln was born on February 12, but he didn't have to be!

SOUL TRAIN

We should also have a Supreme Court for each race.

I'd hate for a bunch of white people to decide whether or not "Soul Train" should stay on the air.

"Sorry. Just not funky enough."

Do you realize there are now white people on "Soul Train" every week? Every week! Just fucking up the show. The train is off the track. Somebody needs to pull the emergency brake. When I was a kid, white people on "Soul Train" were rare, like a funny sitcom. We'd be outside playing; my mother would stick her head out the window. "Come and see this, quick. There's a white girl on 'Soul Train!' " I'd run inside.

ME: Where's she at?

MOM: There she goes.

Now, every week they've got white people on "Soul Train," fucking up the show, slowing down the "Soul Train" dance line.

"Come on, do a split and git."

Once upon a time it was black people on "Soul Train," white people on "American Bandstand."

Those were the rules!

Attention white people: just because your shit got canceled, don't come in and mess up our show, all right?

All right.

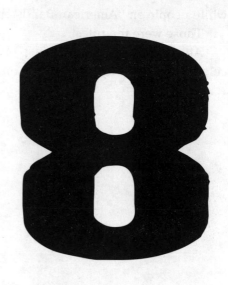

ROCKOLOGY

Popular culture is who we are. It reflects our values, morals, interests, obsessions, ethics, hopes, and dreams.

Man! Are we fucked up? Or just getting bored?

Let's find out.

RAP THIS!

White people don't understand rap.

That's good. It's not for white people.

Anyway, it's not that complicated. Rap is to black people what country music is to whites. Rap is not made for anyone but the people it's made for. When Garth Brooks makes an album, he doesn't stop and think, "Okay, we need something for the black audience." He just makes his records for the country fan. Travis Tritt doesn't think of yuppies, he thinks of cowboy hats.

Same thing with rappers.

White people: the music's not for you.

You can listen, but don't complain.

COUNTRY MUSIC	RAP
Don't care what people think. Only want to please themselves.	Don't care what people think. Only want to please themselves.
Wear jeans and big hats	Wear jeans and big hats
Poor: Come from trailer parks	Poor: Come from the projects
Talk funny, use slang	Talk funny, use slang
Personal, dysfunctional topics	Personal, dysfunctional topics
Cracker music	Nigger music

THE RAP GAP

Every generation says the next generation's music is not as good as theirs. That's wrong, except for my generation's music.

I hate R&B right now. It's not as good as it used to be. Why? Because reading levels are down. You can't read . . . you can't write. How are you going to write a good song if you can't even do "The Alphabet Song" straight through, without mixing up M and N, and forgetting Y?

R&B music these days is almost all about sex. Only Babyface is writing about romance.

And it's all too literal. In the old days, people had metaphors for what they wanted to say. Even the nasty songs aspired to a certain level of craftsmanship. Remember "Pull Up to the Bumper?" For a song about anal sex, it was pretty tongue-in-cheek.

Today, someone would just write a song called "Fuck Me in the Ass."

Music needs to be more vulnerable, but today's artists don't want to be that way. It's not cool. In fact, it's frowned upon in the black community. It's like you're a punk, and young black women want a roughneck. They look on gentleness as a sign of weakness—and next thing you know, art suffers.

There's a big difference between black music videos and white music videos.

Music videos are mostly based on fantasy. But because white people have done almost everything, including become president and gone to the moon, their fantasies are a little more out there. It seems that in white videos there is an endless supply of ideas. You can't predict what you're going to see: a person turning into an egg, then morphing into a church, then falling like strawberry rain.

Black music videos are much more limited, and sad. It's like they have a checklist.

- black leather couch

- Jacuzzi

- nice car

- dancers

- champagne

If these are our fantasies, imagine how we live.

COMEDY WARS

Bad things are happening in rap. Tupac's dead. Notorious B.I.G. is dead. Suge and Puffy are warring. The coasts are at each other's throats.

Could this happen in comedy?

Maybe. Performance vernacular is by nature very violent. "I killed them." "I'm dying up here." "He bombed."

You'd have me and Eddie Murphy on the East coast. Jamie Foxx, Martin Lawrence, and the Wayans brothers on the West.

Adam Sandler and Carrot Top warring. Pauly Shore and Chris Farley facing off. Comics sitting in on other comics' sets, heckling. Coughing during the punchline. Drive-by pie throwing. Or worse: One guy doing the next guy's bit verbatim, just before he can get onstage. Comedy can be cruel.

Fortunately, comedians are not into violence—yet. Gallagher detonating watermelons doesn't count.

BTV

All the blacks I see on TV are so nonthreatening.

It's really sad. What are the networks afraid of? White men's dicks shrinking? White women getting all hot and bothered? Why do we always have to be Jimmy Walker or Urkel? Why aren't there any black Alex Keatons? How come Benson was the smartest black man on TV in the last twenty years?

It's because most TV executives' idea of a black character

is someone mildly retarded. When I first heard about "Homeboys in Outer Space," I thought it was a joke, a bet between two white execs.

EXEC #1: I can get any show on.

EXEC #2: No, you can't.

EXEC #1: I bet I can get a show on called "Homeboys in Outer Space."

EXEC #2: You're on.

A few months later:

EXEC #1: I did it.

EXEC #2: Incredible. So . . . what do you think of "Rednecks in Outer Space?"

I understand why people watched the show. Some viewers can't get enough of TV science-fiction. But going with "Homeboys in Outer Space"? That's like a crack addict so desperate he'll smoke soap.

THE TRUTH ABOUT TALK SHOWS

Why all the fuss about daytime talk shows?

"Lowering our moral standards."

"Perverted."

"Trash TV."

"Where do they get these people?"

Come on. Daytime talk shows are just a cheaper way to do soap operas. It's all the same plot twists.

"Father sleeps with daughter."

"I'm a nun trapped inside a heterosexual man's body."

"My pet and I are in love and living together in sin."

There's no difference between "The Jenny Jones Show" and "General Hospital." It's the same level of dysfunction. Only on "General Hospital" everyone looks nicer, the plots are better, and it costs money. That's the *real* reason we've seen so much trash talk. On soap operas you've got to pay actors and actresses. You need sets. So one day someone said, "Why not let real people do it?"

He was right. Real people are totally the way they seem on daytime talk shows. Everywhere you go there's some fucked-up person waiting for their moment in the spotlight.

I was in the Phoenix airport one time and two girls came up and wanted an autograph. I asked what they were up to.

"We're going to New York to do 'The Gordon Elliott Show.' "

"What's the topic?"

She pointed at her girlfriend. "She fucked my man."

How do they find these people?

You can't blame them. After all, it's $600. Most people need the money. And some serious attention. They might as well get paid for it. So get on a plane. Be special for a day. Be on TV. Be a star to somebody.

Be a star to me.

"Honey? The midget wrestlers who eat snakes from their ass are on next. Oh, and grab me a Pop-Tart, will you?"

NiGHT OF THE LiViNG DEAD

I have my own talk show now—for real. I can interview anyone I want, as long as they're alive. Thing is, I'd like to interview some people who've passed over.

*   *   *

One day years ago I was listening to Redd Foxx on the radio, promoting his one-man show. Then something he said caught my ear.

"Yeah, my favorite young comedian is Chris Rock. He's *real* funny."

Wow. There I was, still living with my mother, and Redd thought I was funny. So I went to the theater, scammed my way in, and got to meet Redd.

Here's what I remember. He had a grenade in his hand—a crystal grenade full of cocaine. He'd click the top and sniff. He also had two or three young women with him. One was a friend of mine's wife. I knew better than to rock the boat.

Redd held out the grenade and said, "You want some?"

ME: No, that's all right.

FOXX: Eh. Good. More for me.

That was it. I would have liked to have a longer conversation. Maybe now I can.

ME: Redd, where you at?

FOXX: In some weird hell.

ME: What do you mean, weird hell? That it looks like the "Sanford & Son" set?

FOXX: No. Every man got his *own* hell. I know this is mine because everywhere I look I see pussy.

ME: And that's hell?

FOXX: Yeah. I can't get none of it.

ME: Are they white girls?

FOXX: They're white, all right . . . because they're covered in cocaine. *The pussy's covered in cocaine and I can't get none of it!*

Sam Kinison was the funniest comedian I ever knew. The first time I saw him at Catch a Rising Star was the hardest I've ever laughed. I walked into the club. I saw Robin Williams, Rodney Dangerfield, and Billy Crystal in the back of the room, watching a guy with a beret. I didn't know why. I found out quickly.

Kinison was great for lots of reasons—and not just because he took me under his wing, was nice to me, and asked me if I wanted to hang out with him at "Saturday Night Live" the evening he got censored for saying that Jesus's last words before being nailed to the cross were, "Ow! Ow! Ow!" I loved Sam because he was just so damn honest. The same as Pryor. In fact, I think he was the white Pryor—the only guy to do something new in the last thirty years. Everyone else is derivative, me included. Eddie does stuff like Pryor, and Pryor's like Cosby. Reiser's like Seinfeld, and Seinfeld's like Klein.

Sam made a lot of questionable moves—like doing *Wild Thing*, trying to be a rock star, and dying young—but he still stood alone. I'd really like to talk with him again.

> ME: Sam, where are you?
> SAM: It looks like heaven. I'm not sure.
> ME: What's it like?
> SAM: Phoenix, with humidity.
> ME: What else?
> SAM: There's pussy everywhere . . .
> ME: All right.
> SAM: It's covered in cocaine.
> ME: Shit . . . ?
> SAM: And I can't get at it. Oh, oh, oh, oh!
> ME: Hey, you see Redd Foxx, say hi.

Sometimes I don't have to imagine conversations with the dearly departed. I was sitting in my office one night just before show time and we had no guest. I don't normally do this in work-related matters, but I started to pray.

"Please, God. Help me out. I need a guest. Send me one. Anyone."

To my surprise, God answered: "Yo, Chris. This is God."

ME: God? Jesus! I mean, God. Hi.

GOD: I heard your prayer. I've decided to help you out.

ME: Thanks, God. But why me?

GOD: I've followed your career. Your comedy is fresh and cre-
ative. You remind me of Kinnison, but you're not self-
destructive. Plus, I really liked you in *I'm Gonna Get You,
Sucka*, when you asked Isaac Hayes, "How much for
one rib?" So your prayer is answered. How would you
like to interview Dr. Martin Luther King, Jr.?

ME: Sure.

GOD: Good. He seemed eager to speak with you, too. He's
already in makeup. I'll let him know.

Later . . .

ME: Hello, Dr. King. What's it like in heaven?

DR. KING: Chris. Hello. Listen, can you tell me what happened
with O.J.?

ME: O.J.? I thought when you're in heaven you know
everything that's going on?

DR. KING: We do. But after the "not guilty" verdict, even God got
sick of O.J. and wouldn't let us watch anymore.

ME: Well, I don't want to disobey the word of God.

DR. KING: Come on, Chris. Could you do that for a brother?

ME: All right. There was a civil trial. They said he was liable. Now O.J.'s got to pay.

DR. KING: How much?

ME: Almost thirty-four million dollars.

DR. KING: Does he get to keep the Heisman?

ME: I don't know. Let's move on. If you had to do it all over
again, would you do anything different?

DR. KING: Check the wire taps. Ha, ha. I don't know. What the
hell was I thinking? I could have spent time with my

185

kids. No, I'm out there marching, and for what? Garbage men? That's what got me killed—all because
those cracker asses didn't want to take a day off. I
needed a day off. Maybe I should have just gotten me
a big church and preached.

ME: What do you think about James Earl Ray saying he
didn't do it and that he wants a new trial? Should he
get one?

DR. KING: Say, Chris, what's up with Dennis Rodman?

ME: What?!

DR. KING: Did you read his book? I love the big type. I also like
his hair. Do you like his hair? You know, eternity is a
long time. I get really bored. I have a high-top fade
now, but I think I'm going to dye it blond tomorrow.
Oh, did I tell you I got an "I've Got a Dream" tattoo?

ME: Do you have wings?

DR. KING: Well, we got the wings, but we don't fly. Most times it
just messes up your back. My back hurts, my feet
hurt. Boy, what I wouldn't do for a good pair of Nikes.
If I could do it all again, I'd have worn some comfortable shoes. My feet are killing me. I'm the only guy in
heaven got to soak his feet every night. I talked to God
about getting a Nike franchise, but there's a lot of red
tape up here. (*pauses*) Say, listen. I got another O.J.
question.

ME: Oh, come on, Dr. King. I can't answer any more questions about O.J.

DR. KING: No, no, no. It's not about the trial. Who do you think
was better? O.J. or Eric Dickerson?

ME: Well, our time's almost up. Thanks for coming on.
Thank God, too. But before we go, tell me: after watching us down here for the last thirty years, any final
thoughts?

DR. KING: Yeah. Tell Halle Berry I said hi.

i'M NOT LAUGHiNG

Sitcom life is nothing like real life.

Only in a sitcom could someone enter a room and you'd never hear it. They do it that way because if you're talking shit about someone, and they sneak up on you, then you're embarrassed and it gets a laugh.

"Pam's a bitch. I don't care. She's a bitch and the next time I see her I'm going to spit in her . . . Hey! Pam. How you doing? We were just talking about you."

Only in a sitcom. When I talk shit about someone, I've got my *eyes on the door.* They should shoot the guy who let that device slip by the first time, because it's ruined many a show.

"Oh, hi? We were just talking about you . . ."

If I could bring back one sitcom for me to star in, it would be "The Jeffersons."

Classic. Revolutionary. There was so much hoopla over "Cosby" and how Cliff Huxtable had money, but George and Louise Jefferson had money way before the Huxtables. When Cliff Huxtable was still in medical school, busing tables, George Jefferson already owned four dry cleaners.

But the best thing about George: he hated white people.

I don't know how they got away with that on national TV. He hated white guys, he hated the interracial couple.

"Damn Dominos."

If they ever do a movie of "The Jeffersons," I want to play George.

THE
NORMAL
GUY

I've been in some movies. I want to make more. But I don't want to be the gimmicky black guy. I'm holding out for something normal. But nothing scares white audiences more than black people being normal.

Please, let me be a normal guy!

I once wanted to read for the Chris O'Donnell role in Al Pacino's *Scent of a Woman*.

They wouldn't let me.

Nothing against Chris O'Donnell, but it would have still been a good movie with me in it. The kid had no parents or girlfriend, so they wouldn't have had to cast any other blacks but me. And think of the sympathy factor: a black kid going to the private school, not having enough money and all.

But they couldn't see it.

Please. Let me be a normal guy!

Hollywood keeps looking for another *Trading Places*. They want something that plays with the black/white differences. I once got a script about a prison screw-up. I'm in a maximum security prison and Dan Aykroyd's in a minimum security prison and there's a paperwork mixup. We end up where we're not supposed to be and the fun ensues. Lots of fun.

I got another script where I talk in Ebonics and a Nick Cage–type guy teaches me to speak right. When I do, I end up taking over the company. Naturally, speaking correctly— speaking white—allows me to fully realize my inherent brainpower.

Hey, let me know when they're remaking *The Prince and the Pauper*.

Please! Let me be a normal guy.

WE
BACK
BLACK

Black people are too accepting of whack black art. Read the review of almost any black movie from any black newspaper, and 99 percent are excellent. No matter how much you like the entire Wayans family, if you print that *Blankman* deserves an Academy Award, why should I believe anything else you say? Dig up a review of Bill Cosby's *Leonard Part 6*. I guarantee you'll find something positive like, "It's great to see a black man making a movie without guns in it." Sounds good, but it's the same thing they said about *Leonard Parts 1–5*. And what about the story? What about the acting? How about the cinematography?

Oh yeah, was it funny?

They don't go into all that because they're just happy a black man made a movie. I am, too, but just making something isn't good enough.

HOW TO
GET A BLACK
MOViE MADE

Getting black films made is tough. Getting good black films made is tougher. The only way for a black man to be in a movie he'd respect is for him to write it himself. Here's what you've got to do.

1. Spend three months to a year writing a script about an idea near and dear to you as a black man. Two weeks after finishing your script, search for black people with money to help you fulfill your dream.

2. After six months of getting doors slammed in your face by record company people, preachers, drug dealers, and any other black people you thought had some money, finally figure out that there's not enough money in the ghetto to get your movie made. Go to Hollywood.

3. Arrive with $500 and a dream. Rent a car. (There goes $350. You're young and black. They want a deposit. Go figure.) Fifteen minutes after leaving the airport, the cops pull you over and beat the shit out of you for being black on a sunny day. Realize you should have gotten on the freeway instead of taking Century Blvd. due east. You're bleeding and roughed up, but your script is unharmed.

4. You try to get an agent and fail. "No one's making black movies now," they all say. So you take your script around to the script-development departments of every major studio in L.A. When you manage to sneak onto the lot, you meet many fine, young development girls (D-girls), all of whom you'd love to score with personally, and probably could, if they weren't trying to sleep their way into being development V.P.s. But everyone is nice and you figure they will get back to you in two weeks, tops. After all, they all said they were looking for a project like yours.

5. Two months later, your five hundred is long gone, you've gotten no call backs, and no dates—except the women you saw during your brief stint as a male escort. Now you're employed in a restaurant. Your self-image has taken a hit because you're a screenwriter reduced to working as a waiter. Who ever heard of such a thing?

6. Two years later. You've been fired from four restaurants—all for the same reason: too busy working on your outside project. Now, you valet park at a hotel. One day, out of sheer frustration, you slip a script into the passenger seat of a black superstar's car. Three weeks later you get a call from that star's office. His assistant read your script and thinks it's the funniest thing. They set up a meeting for Wednesday.

7. When you get there, the fine young assistant asks you if you'd like some coffee or water while you wait. She smiles at you. You feel like a king. She says the star has read your script and thinks it would be a perfect vehicle for him. Everyone in the office loves it, and they just can't wait to make this movie. There's only one catch. You have to rewrite every page.

That's the bad news. But the good news is that they will pay you to do the work. Not a lot of money, but enough for you to quit parking cars for a while.

8. You quit your valet job and tell your boss to kiss your ass. You also make it a point to tell him, "I'm not a valet, I'm a screenwriter." He makes it a point to tell you, "You'll be back."

9. At your studio apartment—really a one-room add-on with a hot plate, behind a garage—you begin to rewrite your movie, happy to be doing what you were born to do. The only problem is you have to hand in every 25 pages to a producer, who scrutinizes them so you can rewrite them again—to his satisfaction—before you go on to the next 25 pages.

10. After three months of writing exactly what the producer told you to write, you meet with the star and he says, "You know what? Something's not right. I like the original better." In fact, they all agree, the original wasn't that far off. He says, "Take a few days to compare the two scripts, make some notes, and call me

Wednesday." As the meeting ends, the producer asks (loudly), "Who told you to write this crap?"

11. Tuesday morning the vice president of development at one of the studios you originally visited three years ago calls. You recognize her voice. She's moved up from D-girl and finally got around to reading your script. She wants to have a meeting tomorrow at 6 p.m. You call up the black star's office to reschedule. There's a problem: the assistant says the star's show has just been canceled and they don't know how long they're going to be in these offices. She's says call her back. You call back in an hour and you get a recording saying the number's disconnected. You're very upset. You were going to ask her out, and now you don't know how to reach her.

12. At the big studio, you meet the V.P. and the head guy. He says he loves your script. It's wonderful! Great! Innovative. There's only one problem. It's too black.

YOU: But it's a movie about Harlem.
STUDIO HEAD: Are there *that* many black people in Harlem?

They pay you money to work with a white writer and make it less black.

13. After a couple months of homogenizing your script, you turn it in. Now, *white* people live in Harlem, only it's not Harlem anymore, it's Cleveland. But the message about people getting along survives, even if it takes a few car chases and gun battles to arrive at it. The studio loves it. You get an agent.

14. Actors are cast. A director is hired. You're supposed to do a final polish, but the director brings in his own writers. You recognize the name of one. Turns out he used to be your boss at the car park. Meanwhile, your new agent negotiates a nice pay off. He also gets you a few gross points on the soundtrack. None is planned, but he still wants to prove he has your best interests at heart. Then he tells you they want you barred from the set.

15. You spend some money on a new apartment—with full kitchen—and start to work on another script which you hope to sell before the money runs out. You also finally feel enough swerve to ask out the development V.P. who brought in your script. But when you call her office, a stranger tells you she's been fired.

16. A year later, the film is released as counterprogramming to the summer blockbuster crush. It does Okay despite going against some big sequels and TV sitcom remakes. However, the hip-hop soundtrack sells like hotcakes and is much bigger than the film. Suddenly you've got bucks deluxe. You're getting calls to do rewrites. Studios want to make deals. Then one day, you find a script in the backseat of your car. . . .

THE KiNG OF QUEENS

Who's been a bigger influence on pop culture for a longer time than Michael Jackson? He was a great black entertainer and now he's a great white entertainer—even though he's still a black entertainer.

But Michael's got problems.

Michael Jackson, the king of pop and biggest-selling artist of all time, almost lost it all.

You know why?

Fooling around with white boys.

I was really hurt when Michael Jackson was charged with child molestation. If it's true, we're all to blame because we saw him with that little kid on his lap at the Grammy Awards. If I'd had a little kid on my lap, they would have had me arrested before they gave out Best Polka Single by an Individual or a Group. But somehow, with a little money and Johnnie Cochran, Michael has remained a free man.

Now Michael has his own child. Prince. Michael was awake and present for the birth, which was tough, because he had never been that close to pussy before. The birth was premature, though. Just like his dad, Prince didn't want to spend any more time inside a woman than he had to.

You know, this whole Michael Jackson thing is only weird if you think he's straight. Consider that for a moment. If I hung out with Liz Taylor, wore makeup, had on eyeliner, what would you think?

"Chris Rock: *gay!*"

Remember when you thought Elton John was straight? It made you scratch your head now and then. It was difficult to accept and understand. Plus, what about the clothes and the feather boas? But now that you know he's not straight, it's easy. It's no problem. I like Elton. I'll go to his concert anytime. He's gay. It all makes sense.

Now Ellen DeGeneres makes sense. I like Ellen. Maybe I'll like her show now, too.

If Michael Jackson would just tell the truth, we could stop being confused. We could let it be.

Little boys on his lap would still have to go, though.

HOLY ROLLING

Everyone in America is looking for God or hiding from him. We're all trying to fill up a spiritual hole.

When I went to church as a kid, I would always fall asleep.

Sorry. My reverend just wasn't that good. The man meant well, but in every field there are just some people who are better than others.

Here was the problem: my reverend had the heart; he just wasn't a great orator. I don't think he could read, either. Every once in a while he would stumble over a passage in the Bible: "A a-b-t-uh, GOD." Or, "I-bl-uh JESUS!"

I never got into religion much. Too many middle men. I love Him but why do I have to talk to God's kid to get to God? Or my reverend? It's like talking to an agent in order to get to the star. I don't want to talk to God's agent or his road manager. I want to talk to God. Any time you go through a middle man, the message gets diluted.

As God says, you want something done right you gotta do it yourself.

When you're black it's hard to latch on to a religion.

There's Christianity. You can't argue with the value system: The Golden Rule and the Ten Commandments.

On the other hand, it's just *so white*.

I know how the leaders might get more black people involved: When they do those new picture bibles, let the people from the Fox Network and UPN do the art.

There's Muslims. They come in all colors and seem very black-friendly. But it can be a little too black for me. I'm looking for a lighter shade of black in my religion. Plus, they're really strict. For instance, if I kill someone in a holy war, I get to go straight to heaven. But if I eat a pork chop, I'm going to hell. That's a little too strict for me. The whole pork thing in general is a bother.

Muslims get to have multiple wives, which is cool. Four wives, eight titties. That'd be great—but I've got to have my bacon.

The coolest thing about Muslims is that they pray five times a day, every day, at the same time. Do you realize how much safer the world would be if we all paused five times a day?

"I'm gonna kill you, motherfucker. I'm gonna kill you—oh, wait a minute. I have to pray."

Afterward: "Now, what were we talking about?"

I know I curse a lot in my act. I talk about sex. No way I can say I'm a very religious person.

But being spiritual is a whole other thing. I definitely believe in some sort of creator. But not for all the reasons everybody else gives. I believe in God because I can't explain man any other way. You can *say* evolution. But how'd the first bit of life get started or get here? Lightning hitting a primordial pool of amino acids and proteins? But how'd the lightning get here?

I'm not doing badly, but I definitely want to live a cleaner and more spiritual life than I am. On the other hand, I don't think I'm going to hell. Jeffrey Dahmer, Manson, Hitler, and O.J. are going to be in hell. I don't think I'll end up with those guys. It's not like in prison, where guys who cheat on their taxes end up in the same cell with murderers. I'm trusting that God is better than the American justice system.

What is hell, anyway? Any place that *isn't* heaven? That's just about everywhere. Bad idea. How about this: if you're reading this book, and it's fun, that's good. But if you had to read this book forever, that would be hell. If you went to Disneyland, it would be fun for a while, but if you stayed forever, you'd wind up chopping off Dumbo's trunk, slapping Mickey and Goofy upside the head, and violating Minnie.

My whole thing about God is simple: I want to find him before he finds me. Usually, when God finds you, it's after you've really fucked up. These days a man will kill his wife, kids, and neighbors, and then say he's found God. I don't think he just "found" him, lying around under some couch. He went after God. Pursued him. Good thing God isn't hard to catch. And being a forgiving God, he'll always take the fuck-up in.

EPiLOGUE

ROCK AND ROLE MODEL

Maybe you liked this book a lot. I hope so. But don't turn me into a role model. You know how I feel about that.

Besides, parents are the only true role models. Good or bad, they're your parents all your life. Their actions will always affect you. Athletes and entertainers are just people who are popular to young people for a while.

I used to like Rick James when I was a kid. Then he did that gold album where he dyed his hair blond. That was enough for me. I turned on him like that. I dropped him like a loose button. The public never supports anyone for an extended period of time who clearly does bad work. Or whack shit. Except Michael Jackson.

If Michael Jordan beat his wife and started smoking crack I would be disappointed, but it wouldn't affect me forever. If he went on TV and *told* people to beat their wives and smoke crack, I would say, "Damn. Michael has lost it." If he started to average four points a game, I'd still have a soft spot for him, but my admiration would move on.

"What happened to that brother?"

"I don't know."

If my father told me to smoke some crack and beat my wife, then I'd be hurt. I'd be damaged.

Heroes come and go: just ask the New Kids on the Block. But your parents are your parents forever. They're who you should look to.

Entertainers aren't role models. You become an entertainer because you *don't* want to get with the norm. That's why there's nothing I hate more than an actor on TV saying, "I try to be good for the kids. I try not to do drugs, for the kids."

I think, "You dumb, ignorant . . . That means if you weren't on TV you would be doing drugs?"

I don't do drugs. You know why? *Because I don't want to. It's just not cool.*

I don't beat women. Why? Because I'm not into that.

It's not because I'm an entertainer.

That's why this whole role model thing bothers me.

Everybody has the potential to be a hero and a role model. Any regular Joe can do it. All the great people in history started out as Joe Blows: Gandhi, MLK, Harriet Tubman, Rosa Parks, Mother Theresa. All normal people, no limelight, and now they're bigger than anything. They never go out of style.

Martin Luther King, Jr., didn't need a big move to the basket. Mother Theresa didn't need Babyface to produce her.

Doing something really profound and personal is bigger than a fad.

Its not some passing fancy.

It's always number one.

Hey, before you go, you gotta hear these messages I got while you were reading:

"Chris. Bill Maher. Just want to say I've loved having you on 'Politically Incorrect' the last few years, especially your election coverage for the show.

"I understand you're scheduled to come on in a few weeks and be on the panel, so like I do for every guest, I just read your book. Frankly, I found it quite disturbing. Your views on racism and women are very, very extreme. Did you actually come up with that stuff yourself? Was this supposed to be a funny book? I only ask because I've written a couple books and I think I have a pretty good idea about what's funny. For instance, that part in I'm Gonna Git You Sucka, when you asked Isaac Hayes, 'How much for one rib?'

"You're not having personal problems, are you? Give me a call when you get to L.A. and we can talk about it."

* Beep *

"It's Lorne Michaels. Say, I got an advance copy of your book and I read it with great interest. However, I must say that it is, without a doubt, at least to me, and I think others will agree, the worst book in the history of literature. As I read your views on popular culture, relationships, race, money, and drugs, I realized I'd never before read a book by someone who had absolutely no idea what he was talking about. Not one thing. You even got the chapter about your mother wrong. I've seen better literature in coloring books.

" 'Saturday Night Live' has turned out some of the biggest stars in the history of comedy: Chevy Chase, John Belushi, Dan Aykroyd, Bill Murray, Eddie Murphy, and more. And after that scene in I'm Gonna Get You Sucka in which you ask Isaac Hayes, 'How much for one rib?' I'm sure you know I'd hoped that you'd take your place among the greats. But none of them has ever done a piece of work this bad. Well, maybe Fletch II, but let's not talk about that now. I think it's more important for you to consider and, I think, accept the fact that with this book coming out soon, your career is all but over.

"That's actually why I'm calling: to let you know that no matter what, there's always a job for you with your friends at 'Saturday Night Live.' Of course, it won't be the same job you had before. I think you can understand, and anyone would agree, that I could never put you on the air again. But how do you feel about mopping floors? Are you any good with machinery? Copy machines? Answering machines? Cappuccino machines? Think it over. And if that doesn't work for you, well, I was at Steve Martin's house the other day and I noticed that a couple of his cars were pretty dirty. You could always give him a call. Let me know what you want to do, and stay well."

* Beep *